BOURNEMOUTH ROCKS!

A Brief History of Rock Music
in Bournemouth, Boscombe & Poole
1960 - 1980

Celebrating many of the groups who played the locality in
their infancy to evolve into Superstars.

Also the musicians living within the County of Dorset
who went on to achieve Local and International fame.

Alan Burridge

Natula Publications

This edition published in 2009 by Natula Publications
Natula Ltd., Christchurch, Dorset BH23 1JD

ISBN 9781897887776

A CIP catalogue record of this book is available from the British
Library.

Printed by Cpod, Trowbridge, Wiltshire.

Preface

Much like vampires, Rock 'n' Rollers usually only come out to play after dark and in this book over 50 groups and artistes who visited venues such as the Bournemouth Hard Rock, the Winter Gardens, Gaumont Theatre, Pavilion Theatre & Ballroom, The Ritz, Chelsea Village and The Village Bowl in Bournemouth, The Royal Ballrooms in Boscombe, The Arts Centre and Technical College in Poole and the numerous fine public houses like The George Hotel, The Old Harry, The Potter's Arms and The Halfway Hotel who supported live music are all remembered. Venues changed their names, as do shops, and Boscombe's Royal Ballrooms was also known as Starkers during this time and is currently called The Opera House. In this book I have called the venue by the name in use at the time of the gig.

Somewhat autobiographical to reflect the flavour of the era, I have looked back at some of the musicians and bands who emerged from the local scene, either just for the love of playing live music like The Push, Abel Cain, Natural Gas and Rock Circus or seeing the dream through to making records such as Spontaneous Combustion, Team Dokus, The Dictators, Infantes Jubilate, Bram Stoker, Elias Hulk and Room. Then there were those who went the extra mile: Zoot Money's Big Roll Band / Dantallion's Chariot, King Crimson, Emerson, Lake & Palmer, The Greg Lake Band, John Wetton with Asia, Andy Summers with The Police, Lee Kerslake with Uriah Heep, and Al Stewart.

Plus there's an extensive listing of groups who visited those venues, in many cases, on their very first UK tour, only to gain more popularity and then move on the play some of the largest and most famous Rock Venues in the World.

The book features: - Mantovani: Six-Five Special: Skiffle: The Shadows: The Beatles: The Rolling Stones: Pick of the Pops: Oh Boy!: Ready, Steady, Go!: Top of the Pops: Radio Luxembourg & The Pirate Radio Stations: Tony Blackburn: Mods, Rockers & Brighton: Willy & The Workers: The Cavaliers: The Small Faces: The Sean Buckley Set: Roy Orbison: The Creation: The Who: The Troggs: The Jimi Hendrix Experience: Pink Floyd: Gene Pitney: Dave Dee, Dozy, Beaky, Mick & Tich: The Walker Brothers: Cat Stevens: Engelbert Humperdinck: The Move: Bram Stoker: The Jeff Beck Group with Rod Stewart: The Dictators: Infantes Jubilate: Brother's Bung: Peter Green's Fleetwood Mac: Simon Dupree & The Big Sound: The Savoy Brown Blues Band: Chicken Shack: The Alan Bown: The Nice: Juicy Lucy: John Mayall's Bluesbreakers: Zoot Money: Andy Summers: Status Quo: The Pretty Things: The Push: King Crimson: Robert Fripp: Unit Four: The Time Checks: Giles, Giles & Fripp: The Shame: Shy Limbs: Emerson, Lake & Palmer: Transit Sound: The Dictators: Spontaneous Combustion: Time: The Greg Lake Band: John Wetton: Al Stewart: Cream: Derek & The Dominoes: Elias Hulk: Room: Yes: The Faces: Thin Lizzy: The Groundhogs: Led Zeppelin: Van Der Graff Generator: Curved Air: Rock Circus: Mugwump: Team Dokus: Natural Gas: Uriah Heep / Lee Kerslake: The Pink Fairies / Russell Hunter: AC/DC: Barclay James Harvest: Blue Oyster Cult: Sight & Sound In Concert: The Old Grey Whistle Test: Climax Blues Band: Dire Straits: Kate Bush: The Punk Era: The Tubes: Blondie: Motorhead.

About the Author

Alan Burridge has been Motorhead's Fan Club Boss since early 1980 and has published over 80 fanzines and 3 books about them. He has written for *Record Collector*, numerous other fanzines and the Internet, album liner notes, novels with his hometowns of Upton and Poole as the backdrop, reviewed well over a hundred gigs for Mr. Kyps live music venue, is a Top 500 reviewer for Amazon, and veteran of Express FM's *Write On* radio show.

http://www.alanburridge.freeuk.com

Dedication

This book is dedicated to Eric Billett and Eddie Evans, two great friends and brothers in my love for rock music, who between them have accompanied me to most of these gigs.

Also to Dave Robinson, a more recent and third great friend and brother, whose Bourne Beat Bar is a massive tribute to Bournemouth's vibrant music scene and its fans.

Introduction

1960 to 1980 was a fantastic era, perhaps we didn't regard it as such at the time as it was evolving around us, but with the benefit of retrospect then yes, it was.

The Second World War began on September 3rd 1939 and ended on September 2nd 1945; I was born just 6 years later. By 1957 when Skiffle began, followed by the equally outrageous Rock 'n' Roll our parents and grandparents must have wondered if they really had done the right thing by winning the war. They were accustomed to the somewhat restful music of the post-war year's 'Easy Listening' and that of the pre-war 'Swing Era'; the music of Mantovani, Glenn Miller and Billy Cotton and singers like Vera Lynn, Nat King Cole and Frank Sinatra, so this upsurge of what many regarded as 'The Devil's Music' didn't go down very well.

Both the stars and their fans of this new radically outrageous and noisy music were part of the first two non-conformist generations who had decided to uproot and turn on its head the then stolidly laid down codes of dress, attitude and hair cut, and coupled with the need to do things our own way; upon hindsight, I suppose we had a bit of a cheek. So it is no wonder we were ridiculed for our beliefs by the older generations, taunted for being effeminate due to the length of our hair, chastised and rebuked for our dress sense, our anti-establishment attitudes, general rebellion and counter-culture stance simply because we wanted to be 'different'.

Although they eventually, albeit begrudgingly, began getting used to the music and fashion revolution surrounding them after years of nothing but Armed Forces Uniforms and pin-striped 'de-mob' suits, those relations and onlookers found us very difficult to warm to, and with our flowing shoulder-length locks, crushed velvet 22" bell-bottomed 'hipster' trousers in quite outrageous colours, multi-coloured or floral-print shirts and frock-tailed 'Doc Holliday' jackets was it any wonder? We were indeed 'dandies' and 'dedicated followers of fashion', but in the Summer of '67 we would evolve into hippies and become an integral part of yet another revolution, this time aimed at 'Peace and Love', which must have pleased them just a little bit, surely? The obligatory 2 years of National Service or conscription had only stopped in 1960, so both the Armed Forces and our relations probably shuddered to even consider what might happen should the country ever need defending again - by the likes of us.

But conscription *had* ended and the music of this revolutionary era also shaped our lives and helped change the outlook of the older generations as well as our own, and indeed, some of the songs which were scorned at the time are now looked back upon in hindsight with an extreme degree of fondness and affection.

A myriad of groups and artistes were playing the numerous venues tucked within the seaside towns of Bournemouth, Boscombe and Poole and in the years since, I have had within me the passion to try and catalogue this amazing era for future generations' reference. As ever in our hurried lives, it has been a case of finding the time to get this information exorcised from within and written down; so after calling upon the many notes and scribblings made over the years, and delving deep into the currently rather exceptionally good memory, the spare time Christmas and New Year 2007 had on offer just happened to fit the bill to enable the main bulk of the progress to be made.

Within these pages are reviews of the bands and artistes I was fortunate enough to see for myself, but there were a great many more which, usually due to an unfortunately shallow pocket, I couldn't. However, it is hoped that this short journal will be of interest to the Bournemouth area beat and rock enthusiast; *they were* very interesting and radical times, *they were* very interesting and radical musicians and I hope I have captured the essence of the period.

Alan Burridge. 2009.

Bournemouth Rocks!

Whilst Bournemouth may be constantly ridiculed as a refuge for senior citizen retirement similar to Eastbourne, The Isle of Wight, or Cornwall, it has always been thoroughly alive and kicking as far as the night-life is concerned and has produced more than a few famous personalities as well as some of the already famous deciding to live here. With venues to suit bands starting out on the ladder to fame and those at the top of their profession, it has always been one of the main South Coast locations where the majority of groups across the decades had a date to play in Bournemouth on their nationwide tour itinerary.

Mantovani.

Okay, I'm aware that singer and entertainer, Max Bygraves, 'Wakey-Wakey' band leader, Billy Cotton (1899-1969), and light orchestra leader and conductor, Mantovani, had homes in the posh areas around Bournemouth such as Canford Cliffs, Branksome and Sandbanks, and they may well have been what we regarded as 'square' man, but the town also had a bit of Rock 'n' Roll about it when in 1965, Beatle, John Lennon, bought his Aunt Mimi a bungalow at 126 Panorama Road, Sandbanks for £25,000, which he and Yoko Ono would often visit, also using it as a hideaway and bolt-hole from their hectic London lifestyle.

And it wasn't due to the fact Mantovani had a home in the area that my parents wanted to attend when he and his orchestra played Bournemouth's Winter Gardens, probably in about 1958 or 1959. Annunzio Paolo Mantovani (1905-1980) was the U2 of his day, perhaps even bigger, as he had about 50 albums released in the UK with 40 of them also out in America. In fact, Mantovani sold more records than anyone else in his day - until The Beatles came along.

Max Bygraves spoke on local TV about his 'mansion' costing in the region of £350,000 when he bought it in the 50s. Mantovani's 'pad' would have been in much the same category, perhaps worth even more, so plainly this 'crooner / big band / light orchestra' era, which ended its dominance when Rock 'n' Roll began with the likes of Elvis Presley (1935-1977), Bill Haley (1925-1981), Buddy Holly (1936-1959) and Little Richard was more than capable of making millionaires when comparisons are made to the present day monetary value. But, with Rock 'n' Roll waiting in the wings to impress the then younger generation, namely *us,* those stars were, despite the fact they didn't know this radical change was just around the corner, making hay whilst the sun still shone.

The Winter Gardens, Bournemouth

Unlike some parents of today, though, mine didn't palm my brother and I off with Gran, Auntie or whomever when they wanted to attend a local event. And despite the equally expensive ticket prices in comparison to a man's wage at the time, somehow they managed to afford it and took us with them. (Mum was thrifty but the trade-off would be suffering *The Sound Of Music* somewhere in the future, and I know millions of people will disagree as they love it, but for me it was like *The Waltons* would turn out to be, perfect family life and mine had been nowhere near it. Don't get me wrong, we were not brought up badly, by and large we treated very well, but father was a very hard taskmaster, and with my 'rebel' instincts we simply didn't get on). And whilst racking up royalties from the release of those 50 or so albums, Mantovani's greatest hit was an instrumental, as were all of his tunes, called *Charmaine*. It was and still is to Mantovani what *Stairway To Heaven* is to Led Zeppelin - his signature tune; his song which had to be played at every concert. And I must say those orchestral, cascading strings that were his trademark somehow tugged at every sensation within the human psyche, and you had to be an absolute plank not to be emotionally charged with adrenaline upon hearing that fantastic tune.

Mantovani was an absolute god of his era!

'Six-Five Special' & Skiffle.

Not many people owned a television in the late 1950s, but Granddad Walter Burridge did and it was a massive piece of kit with a fairly small black and white picture in the centre of a huge grey screen, bought during the 1953 'TV Boom' created by people wanting to watch The Queen's Coronation. As a family, we would visit him on a Saturday evening to watch *Dixon of Dock Green*, but also managed to see the last 15 minutes or so of what was probably the first pop TV programme ever, called *Six-Five Special*, with Pete Murray and Freddie Mills as the hosts. (Local folklore has it that Freddie Mills began his boxing career at Poole Fair, which is always held in November and is notorious for always raining when the tents and attractions are pitched there.) The theme tune went something like *The Six-Five Special's running down the line, Freddie Mills got left behind* ... or was that something we made up as school kids?

After seeing active service in the trenches during World War I, Granddad had been, out of necessity more than choice, a policeman during World War II and thereafter a carpet fitter and master-carpenter for the Poole High Street shop named Butlers, situated where Burger King now stands. *Dixon of Dock Green* was a BBC TV crime drama about Police Constable George Dixon, played by Jack Warner (1897-1981) and might well have been Granddad's favourite, but *Six Five Special* was also the favourite of his youngest son, my Uncle Les, and it would soon became mine.

Six-Five Special, so named as it was broadcast at five minutes past six, was launched in 1957, and it introduced the younger generation to a style of music which quickly became known as Skiffle. The man who would achieve lifelong fame and eventual legendary status as the 'King of Skiffle' was Lonnie Donegan, whose *Rock Island Line* single, written by blues man, Huddie 'Lead Belly' Ledbetter (1888-1949) originally brought to prominence by the Johnny Cash imported American recording, spent an unprecedented 8 months in the British Top 20 and quickly became Donegan's signature tune. Lonnie

4

Donegan and Skiffle were an almost unintentional by-product really, as the show mainly featured older and more boring acts (by younger generation standards anyway) like Cleo Laine, Johnny Dankworth and Petula Clarke. Now and again, though, an outrageous act like Wee Willie Harris would make an appearance and the parents and grandparents would be outraged because Pete Murray had told us (and with the picture being in black and white he'd had to) that Wee Willie's hair was dyed yellow and green. This was something of a thrill, not only because Wee Willie had been so outrageous, but because he had annoyed the elder generations by being that way, and after the strict disciplines they had suffered from fighting in two World Wars, rebellion like this, which was hardly masculine, was looked upon as 'Well, if there is another war, what will we do with our soldiers looking like that and dancing about as if they've got ants in their pants?' So this new 'Pop(ular) Music' was being looked upon as something quite disgraceful, with most ex-forces men spitting upon its name with more than a great deal of contempt. (Wee Willie Harris had hits with *Lollipop Mama* and *Digging' My Potatoes* amongst others in the late 1950s and he is still playing on the revival circuit today).

Whilst along with Bert Weedon, Hank Marvin of The Shadows would later be credited for prompting teenagers to buy themselves a red-bodied Fender Stratocaster guitar and learn how to play it, likewise, Lonnie Donegan inspired the youth of the UK to start a Skiffle group. On the face of it, this appeared quite a simple thing to do, all they needed was an acoustic guitar, someone who could sing, a washboard and thimbles, and a double bass made from a tea chest, a broom stick and a piece of thick rope or string.

Skiffle moved the popular music goalposts away from the orchestras and the orchestra-backed singers like Frank Sinatra, Perry Como and Mario Lanza, and gave the opportunity of being a 'star' to the ordinary teenagers from the streets of the post-war UK's towns and cities. In doing so, it just preceded Rock 'n' Roll in fulfilling this role of giving a genre of music to the younger generation, instead of, as it had been, strictly for the middle-aged and older performers and their audiences.

Uncle Les, 10 years older than me, would thoroughly enjoy this programme. He would often be sitting there with his Poole Grammar School classmate and pal, Brian 'Dilly' Downer, enjoying *Six-Five Special* as then and even now, it was 'cool' to know what was going on in the 'Pop Charts'. On other occasions, Les and Dilly would have the record player out to play their records, introducing everyone in the family, whether they liked it or not, to the world of Skiffle, by blasting out those such as the aforementioned *Rock Island Line* and perhaps *Singing The Blues* which had been a No.1 hit for Tommy Steele in 1956, amongst many others.

The Pavilion, Bournemouth

Uncle Les was and still is quite a rock 'n' roller. A great Buddy Holly fan, just 11 months before 'The Day The Music Died', on March 22nd, 1958, he cycled the 8 miles from Upton to Bournemouth, then caught a bus to Salisbury to see the Buddy and The Crickets gig at The Gaumont Theatre; arriving back at home around 2am. Of course, he attended other concerts by The Everly Brothers, Little Richard, Bill Haley and many others at The Winter Gardens as and when the tours brought those stars closer to home.

The Gaumont (now the Odeon cinema), Salisbury

But despite the magic of Mantovani being the first ever concert I attended in Bournemouth, and both parents enjoying some of his 78rpm records and LPs frequently, I was a bit too young to fully appreciate Lonnie Donegan and Skiffle at the time but it would be the sound of the guitar which captured both my heart and imagination when I first heard records by -

The Shadows.

Like every large town bordering upon city status, Bournemouth has, from the late 1950s right through to the present day, been host to the majority of the major pop and rock tours of the day with stars ranging from Gene Vincent (1935-1971), Lonnie Donegan, The Beatles and The Rolling Stones right through to Take That, Oasis, 50 Cent and The Pussycat Dolls playing venues within the town and in 1960 or 1961, The Shadows would prove to be no exception.

As kids we would listen to the BBC Light Programme's *Uncle Mac's Children's Favourites* on the radio. The much-requested tunes included: *The Laughing Policeman* recorded in 1922 by Charles Penrose (1873-1952), it sold over a million copies; Michael Holliday's (1924-1963) *The Runaway Train* (No.24 September 1956) and perhaps the absolutely dire American song released in 1947 called *Sparky's Magic Piano*. Uncle Mac (Derek McCulloch OBE 1897-1967) would also play *Last Train To San Fernando* by Johnny Duncan & The Blue Grass Boys or The Goon's *Ying-Tong Song*, which went down a little bit better, and occasionally a record by The Shadows. My first record of theirs (a 45) was *Guitar Tango* and their second, an adrenaline-pumping tune called *Apache*, would become their signature tune.

If The Shadows were not already huge stars in their own right as Cliff Richard's backing band, then they soon would be. After hearing Jerry Lordan's demo for the *Apache* instrumental, Cliff's EMI producer, Norrie Paramor, decided they should record their own tunes, high-pitched and twiddley in direct contrast to those chunky, American, bass string driven instrumentals such as *Rebel Rouser* and *Peter Gunn* by Rock 'n' Roll guitarist Duane Eddy, which were starting to become popular, and *Apache* would ensure they truly were when it reached No.1 in July 1960. They would continue to be an extremely popular international act on the touring circuit for the next 40 years or more. The Shadows or more especially their lead guitarist Hank B. Marvin, in the meantime, would inspire thousands of teenagers to learn to play the guitar and form a group of their

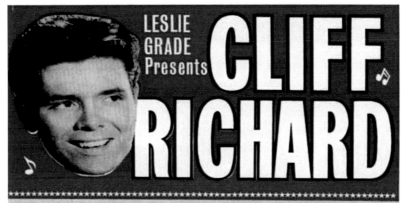

Poster for Cliff Richard and The Shadows Concert
The Gaumont, Bournemouth on 2nd – 4th August 1965
Courtesy of the Bourne Beat Bar, Bournemouth

own. And a great many young British bands started with the Hank Marvin (lead), Bruce Welch (rhythm guitar), Jet Harris (bass guitar) and Tony Meehan (drums) format. Most had not only fallen in love with The Shadows' guitar-driven sound, but also the sound of Hank's red *Fender Stratocaster* guitar. In years following he would also use a *Burns* guitar for a while, but *'The Strat'* would become his trademark as time and their career progressed.

I don't know how we found out that they were playing at The Winter Gardens (the local paper perhaps or because Dad worked in Bournemouth and had seen a poster?) or how our parents afforded the tickets but they took us to see them. It proved to be something quite different to the Mantovani experience. Whereas his orchestra was un-amplified loud, from which you heard the natural sound of the instruments, and it must be borne in mind there were quite a lot of them in an orchestra but The Shadows were but four people, with three of them using, much to my father's alarm and horror (and which by today's standards would be laughable), Vox AC30 30 watt amps and a *very* small public address system.

Mum, my brother Robert and I enjoyed this LOUD music by The Shadows, but father spent the whole show, which must have lasted for at least an hour if not 90 minutes, with his fingers pushed firmly into his ears almost screaming in horror! We thought this was extremely funny until the 1990s, when he received a War Pension after finding out that he had sustained hearing damage from the non-stop bombardment at El Alamein, in North Africa, where he had been posted during World War II. Needless to say, father did not attend any more live concerts with amplified guitars and was loath for me to do so, too.

The Beatles & The Rolling Stones.

Bursting as the music scene was at the time with new talent from The Beatles and The Rolling Stones, the daily newspapers tended to brand them as 'long-haired, scruffy individuals who don't wash' and of course, parents believed it impressing the assets of cleanliness upon us all the more. It wasn't 'the thing' to be seen or heard glorifying this rebel/rabble uprising of youth, and anyway, it wouldn't last would it; just a five-minute wonder that would soon go away?

Yeah, right!

Once a fortnight, we would walk the mile or so to visit Gran's sister, Auntie Doris, who lived in one of the Lady Wimborne houses not far from St. Michael's church in nearby Hamworthy. Married to Uncle George (who looked very much like 'Sunny Jim' on the Force Wheat Flakes cereal packets), they had a daughter and son-in-law in Auntie Beryl and Uncle Bob respectively. Their daughter, Pamela, our cousin was also in our age group.

My brother Robert and I never got on with Pam; she was an only child and could and did have everything she wanted, and quite opposite to us, was completely spoilt. And of course, Pam had none of the restrictions we suffered, like we daren't mention The Beatles or The Stones or even breathe we knew their names; yet Pam suddenly had all of The Beatles singles, and would be playing them time and time again when we visited.

Although four years older than me, Robert didn't get bitten by the Rock 'n' Roll bug, whilst I did, so I used this time with cousin Pam to listen and learn what The Beatles really were all about, and why their music was causing such a stir. And agreed, it was different, it wasn't Mantovani, The Shadows, Johnny Duncan, or indeed even Lonnie Donegan; it was something completely new and radical!

With almost a lifetime to work it out, I suppose the bitter pill we had to swallow was that Auntie Beryl and Uncle Bob would just go out and buy Pam two or three 45s without even thinking about it. They were 6 shillings and 8 pence each (6/8d is about 33 pence today) and simple mathematics says you could get 3 for £1; but when a grown man earned between £4 and £7 per week, it was a lot to pay out on 3 records. It took 2 weeks delivering the evening paper in all weathers to earn myself a £1 and at that age I had yet to learn to *admire* Pam for her cunning and good luck at being an only child. Instead I was filled with bitterness, resentment, jealousy and envy, which are negative emotions whereas admiration is positive and good for the body and soul. But when I *could* actually afford a 45, which wasn't very often, it was something quite marvellous, and buying it gave a great feeling of achievement, yet with Pam's parents buying them almost willy-nilly, perhaps hers didn't mean quite as much or were not as precious and hard-won as mine?

To combat this expense, we used a second-hand reel-to-reel tape machine Mum had bought for a couple of quid from a friend named Pam Warren, to record our favourites from Alan 'Fluff' Freeman's (1927-2006) Sunday afternoon BBC radio show *Pick Of The Pops* (which started in 1955 on the BBC's Light Programme and was introduced by David Jacobs). This was about the best we could do but 'Fluff' was consistently very annoying as he'd 'talk-over' the beginnings and endings of the records which would spoil the tape. Of course, this ensured that we would have to go out and *buy* a copy instead of home-recording it, but as there were so many records we liked compared to how little money we had it was simply a case of recording them and having to put up with Fluff's voice spoiling things. Such was life, but I can't see today's teenager's doing such a thing. Nowadays they just pay for a 'download' if they want a record; how times and technology have changed!

But let's get back to the 1960s and at dinner that evening when Mum told Dad how 'off-the-rails' Pam was becoming listening to music by those dirty long-hairs The Beatles, it was far safer just to nod your head and agree when Dad told us we would never buy a Beatles record *or* grow our hair long.

Deep down inside, though, I couldn't wait to do just those things!

And our generation, who just happened to be one of the first post-World War II generations who would escape conscription, were also to grow our hair long in direct contrast to and in defiance of all the men who had fought and died for their Country, OUR Country, and we were regarded as dirty filthy beatniks just like The Beatles and The Rolling Stones, who were now our heroes, and not only that, we wanted to dress and look just like they did, too!

Nevertheless, Cousin Pam offered a first taste of The Beatles and for that I will be forever grateful. It wasn't her fault she had easy-going parents and had they not been so I wouldn't have known anything about The Beatles music for quite some time. The newspapers favoured The Beatles slightly more than The Rolling Stones, as the Stones were regarded more the beatnik type which, upon hindsight is surprising, because they came from a more upper-class, (Richmond in London) background than The Beatles, who had grown up in the backstreets of Liverpool.

Mostly, though, we were a brand new generation, and a generation whom, after our parents and grandparents being a part of and winning our freedom during the hardships of both World Wars, were regarded as 'ungrateful' by not conforming to the short-back-and-sides hairstyle they had been forced to suffer in the conscripted Armed Forces and also begrudged the freedom we had and the way, in their eyes at least, we were abusing it. As far as they were concerned, we were 'youth gone mad'!

Oh Boy & Ready, Steady, Go!

Although *Six-Five Special* had been the voice of teenage youth in the late 1950s, it was closely followed by *Oh Boy*, upgraded by producer, Jack Good, from the remnants of *Six-Five Special*, which made Cliff Richard & The Shadows (who, with The Vernon Girls, had a residency on the show) household names and massive stars. *Ready Steady Go* came along on ITV in 1963 with presenters Keith Fordyce and Cathy McGowan. Broadcast on a Friday evening, its more easy-going nature was designed to rival the BBC's more staid and starchy *Top of the Pops*.

Ready, Steady, Go, or 'RSG' as it later became known, focused more on the evolving 'Beat Music', a name probably taken as much from the 'beat' of the music as from the 'beatnik' name we were being tagged with. But very few homes had the luxury, as it was regarded then, of owning a TV, and even though a few class mates from school would be talking about these programmes, without the necessary TV set it was no more than just a mythical rumour.

The Beat Groups and Stars they featured on 'RSG' would be The Who, The Small Faces, Dusty Springfield, The Kinks, The Beatles, Them, The Rolling Stones and Cilla Black amongst others but my memory has no recall of ever seeing *Ready Steady Go* although I must have done so as it ran from August 1963 until December 1966 and I definitely watched Jimi Hendrix on his debut *Top of the Pops* show in the September. The reason must have been that TV was regarded as much of a time-waster as it is now and since we had so many jobs to do in the home and garden at that time watching *Top of the Pops* was regarded as my quota for the week.

Top of the Pops.

The BBC started broadcasting *Top of the Pops* in 1964, when I was 13 and very impressionable. At school (Lytchett Minster Secondary Modern, which was also known as 'The Manor' because the main building had been one in the past to Sir Thomas and Lady Lees and their family), Friday morning lessons were known as Rural Science which translated as plain old honest-to-goodness gardening. As the area was part of a rural Dorset community, most families had large gardens or smallholdings as they were more familiarly known at the time and we had grown up planting spuds, cabbages, runner beans and other produce. In those days, without the now taken-for-granted motorways, (and with the Country still recovering from the war and rationing) food could not be transported as fast as it is today and would be rotten by the time it reached the local shops if it travelled some distance by rail or road, so everyone grew their own. It was much the same with eggs, so each family had their own chickens and or bantams in the back garden plot.

So, the boys were taught Rural Science on a Friday morning whilst the girls studied Domestic Science, which was just a fancy name for cookery, and as we had to learn how to plant and grow food for the family to eat, so too the girls had to learn how to cook and present it. Today's everyday phrases like 'fast food' and 'take-away' had yet to be introduced into the English vocabulary.

Still, we didn't have a TV.

TV was a rich man's luxury at the time and had yet to be affordably mass-produced, and even so, the picture was in black and white; colour was just something that might happen one day in the future, perhaps?

And during Rural Science, some of the other lads whose families owned or had access to a TV set, would be talking about the groups they'd watched on *Top of the Pops* the evening before. Once again, it confounded me as we didn't have a television and it wouldn't have been the thing to do especially as all the groups on programmes like *Top of the Pops* were regarded as almost anarchic by parents and grandparents alike, to have asked Granddad, who still had that TV we'd watched *Six-Five Special* on, if I could watch *Top of the Pops*?

So I just listened to and asked questions about the programme from these class mates who had seen it, and they were mainly Eric

Billett, Peter Stickland and Kevin Hannam; who had learned to play instruments and also 'played some Shadows songs' onstage at Lytchett Matravers village hall. Eric had been the drummer, having borrowed some old-fashioned style of kit from his granddad; Kevin played rhythm guitar and Peter, lead. But there was already minor skirmishes within the band as Kevin was better at playing chords *and* lead and had been relegated to rhythm as Pete, at the time, wasn't so good with the chords, but had taken the 'starring role' of playing the Hank Marvin's lead melody lines, which were obviously the best parts to play.

So, the four of us lads had The Shadows in common and somehow they managed to see *Top of the Pops* every week and I'd hear different names like The Who, The Pretty Things, and again, The Beatles and The Rolling Stones and so on. But gradually 'Pop Music', much to our elders' disappointment, was catching on and The Beatles especially were starting to sell previously unprecedented amounts of records both in the UK and America. After all, the BBC and ITV were reflecting the changing times by giving half-an-hour a week to the music the UK's youth wanted to hear. And then, more so than ever before, the weekly 'charts' became the talking point of the younger generation, as we would be expected to know whose records were in the charts, and more importantly, who was at Number One?

And so, somehow I would latch on to and get a Friday morning Rural Science job in the school walled garden with Eric, Kevin or Pete and bleed them dry asking questions about *Top of the Pops*. And within it, one of them would say something about this group of theirs, even though it didn't seem as if they played that many gigs; and I learned, not only that Kevin and Pete owned Watkins Rapier guitars (a fairly good replica of Hank Marvin's Fender Stratocaster but less expensive) but they also needed a bass player.

Eric told me playing bass was okay but it was boring, but to be honest I didn't care; I had loosely been told by the three of them that if I could get hold of a bass guitar and what passed for an amplifier in those days, then I was in. Even though I had never yet seen The Who, and from their description they sounded the ideal band for me, I wanted to play in a band like nothing else in the world mattered; but how could I begin to even consider affording a guitar and an amplifier? Neither could any of my family, we were just everyday Upton village folk. Then Pete and Kevin told me about a guitar shop in Westbourne, in Bournemouth, called Don Strike, who not only *sold* guitars but also sold *the parts to make them with!*

So, to cut a long story short, I started making a bass and then Eric, Kevin and Pete decided they weren't going to play or be a band any more. So, I cut the fret board down to make it six-string guitar size, and after several attempts had an electric guitar to play the melody line to Frank Sinatra's *Strangers In The Night* and with a lot of help from Kevin and Pete, and our Lytchett Manor ex-jazz pianist teacher, Neil Sagar, managed to pass CSE Music.

Radio Luxembourg & The Pirate Radio Stations.

In the event of there being no TV set in a home, most of our age group cleverly asked for the then fairly new and battery operated 'transistor radios' for either Birthday or Christmas presents. Discretely, under the sheets and blankets of our bed, this new teenage rebel generation could tune into and enjoy Radio Luxembourg, which played a great many of the singles from the UK charts. Then, when 'pirate radio stations' came on the air, parents and grandparents believed our generation had 'completely taken leave of their senses' and had been 'absolutely anarchic thinking they could do such a thing in complete defiance of the BBC!'

In 1964, pirate radio stations started broadcasting from ships anchored just beyond the obligatory 3 miles offshore limit, where they were regarded as being in 'international waters'. So the likes of the BBC and the Government, who were totally opposed to the pirates, were objecting to them as they were not paying any fees to broadcast, were stealing listeners away from the BBC and playing some of the records far too often. The BBC had always adopted a policy against what would come to be known as 'plugging a record' (playing a record too frequently and thus swaying the record sales towards it) by any particular artiste, as this could lead to their DJs being discretely paid 'a back-hander' to 'plug or push' certain groups or artistes. Plus, the pirate disc jockeys spoke to their audience in a much more informal manner; the younger generation had had enough of listening to the BBC's announcers 'speaking with a plum in their mouth'.

Radio Caroline   **Radio London**

Eventually, of course, the main culprits operating these pirate radio stations, Radio Caroline and Radio London, would be closed down by Government legislation, but nevertheless they had turned the trick as the staid and old-fashioned BBC would be forced to reinvent itself, not only by originating its own 'pop radio station' with Radio 1, but also by employing some of those pirate radio DJs such as Tony Blackburn, Johnny Walker, John Peel and Dave Cash as its disc jockeys, who had already become favourites of the pirate stations' listeners, and would thus sway them back towards listening to Radio 1.

One particular 'under the bedclothes' single plugged on Radio Caroline, was *My Friend Jack* by The Smoke. With its hook-line of *My friend Jack eats sugar lumps* the BBC refused to play it by claiming it would, "corrupt the younger generation with its drug connotations," because, or so they said, "the younger generation took liquid LSD by swallowing it on a sugar cube." This, however, begs the question: How did the old farts at the BBC have knowledge of hard drug usage? Well, they taught me something by banning The Smoke's record, I'd just liked the song for the weird guitar sound, but now they'd told me how to take LSD!

In 1965 when I was 14 we finally had our own TV. This was great, and with just BBC 1, BBC 2 and ITV to choose from *Top of the Pops* was mine, and with luck, anything else pop orientated. Much like any new technology, though, TV became a fascination for the whole family at the outset before settling into the routine of the just about bearable *Sunday Night at the London Palladium* and the absolutely dire *Black & White Minstrel Show*. Rather than watch some of that awful stuff, I would just go to my bedroom (shared with brother Robert) and play records or write stories, lyrics, poetry or just gibberish.

Willy & the Workers and The Cavaliers.

Willy & The Workers were the first band I ever heard rehearsing. They did so at the Upton Church Hall and could plainly be heard from our back garden. Dad would mutter something like, "They'll all end up deaf!" but I would have loved to walk up the road and gone in just to watch. The 'Behind-the-scenes' world of a band had fascinated me since The Shadows gig. Most people took seeing a band or artiste onstage at face value: they bought a ticket, they went, they watched, and then they went home; but I had wondered where the band had suddenly appeared onstage from? How had they travelled to the gig? Where had they played yesterday? Where would they be playing tomorrow? Where would they be staying over-night and so on?

At that time, bands were advertised on a poster outside the venue or in *The Evening Echo* so we knew nothing about any other places they were playing or that it was part of a nation-wide tour; they played Bournemouth or Poole and that was all we knew. Some years later, after thinking the bands were sitting at home with their feet up after their single and album had dropped out of the charts and they had toured the UK I realised they were touring Europe, Scandinavia, and for some, America. I didn't realise how hard the bands were worked by their record company and management but our world was a much smaller place then and anything outside the Bournemouth and Poole area seemed like a foreign land but times have changed, drastically.

Willy & The Workers were some older lads from school. Roger Taylor, who was known around the village of Upton for his musicianship, was The Worker's guitarist, Alan Brown, known as 'Hovis', played bass and 'General' John Fancy was the drummer or another guitarist. The music scene was still tainted with this 'beatnik' image; when young and impressionable kids like myself were told that we should avoid any contact with them as they were regarded as 'never-do-wells', I was far too young to even consider asking if I could go to see a group on my own. It was a 'no-go' area and not even worth asking, despite the fact I had a gut feeling that I would enjoy everything to do with that kind of lifestyle.

Similarly, in our locality, The Cavaliers were the most famous band on the local circuit at the time and with Mum working at the village shop, she would often bring home tales of her colleague, Joan Whitlock and husband, Paul, going to see them at some pub or other, like The World's End at Almer. Their name was massive on a local scale as a 'must-go-and-see' band, and they had an excellent reputation playing venues mainly around Dorset and the West Country. I believe their full name was The Cavalier's Show Band.

Mods, Rockers & Brighton.

By now we were winning some respect from our elders at our stance to be different and, subconsciously, I think it was due to our effort at burying the war years and trying to bring some vitality, hope and freshness back into our country.

And then the fights began between the Mods and the Rockers, usually on Bank Holiday weekends on the seafront at South Coast towns such as Brighton, which knocked us right down again. During these fights the Rockers often used their motorcycle chains and flick-knives as weapons, but the Mods were by no means innocent either! And the news media made such a huge, headline-grabbing outrage of it by saying things like, "This is what happens when conscription stops and young people are given a free reign." So for a short while we had to put up with embarrassment on behalf of our peer Mods' and Rockers' behaviour and look upon it as a reprimand, as we were all tarred with the same damned brush.

Parents and grandparents almost laughed in our faces at this turn of events, "Look what a mess you're making of things now you're standing on your own two feet. We fought the Hun, all you lot can do is fight one another!" We deserved it. The Mods with their parkas, Lambrettas and suits and the Rockers with their black leather jackets, motorcycles and oily jeans were each others' own worst enemies and in these Bank Holiday fights and riots the new culture we were trying to bring into everyone's lives with our new music and this stance at dragging our backsides out of the depressing war years was set back and almost trodden upon like a well-smoked dog-end. Yes, both sides were fighting for their own 'rights' as were our parents and grandparents during those war years, but they were fighting *an enemy;* we (our generation) were fighting *each other!* What a bunch of idiots! We deserved the looks of contempt we were given and gradually we had to heal those wounds and fight for *the right cause* again, together!

The Small Faces.

Just before leaving school, my cousin Richard and I went to see The Small Faces. Bournemouth's Gaumont cinema had just started featuring 'pop groups' to get a foothold on this up-and-coming 'scene' to make some money before it disappeared as the 'fad' they thought it would be. Steve Marriott and the band had fast become very popular with their Decca singles and *Top of the Pops* appearances, (with *Whatcha Gonna Do About It* and *Sha-La-La-La-Lee*) and were quite a favourite with virtually everyone. The Support band, Richard remembers but doesn't know why, was the Sean Buckley Set, who were obviously good enough for their role in the scheme of things, but not destined for stardom.

The Beatles and The Rolling Stones had also played The Gaumont in 1962 and 1963 and the local paper made a big thing about it, absolutely outraged that local youngsters could become caught up in what was now being called 'Beatle-Mania' with teenage girls crying hysterically at their idols, and screaming until they were either sick, hoarse, or both. Family friend, John Bongard told of his father being a policeman at the time and having to help 'smuggle' The Beatles into the Gaumont's stage door in an ice cream van in an effort to throw the screaming fans off their track (they had a week's residency at the venue in November 1963) and thus allowing them to actually gain entry to the building to play their shows.

Roy Orbison.

A while later, Roy Orbison (1936-1988) or 'The Big O' was top of the bill over The Small Faces on the strength of his No.1 record *Oh, Pretty Woman* and he was great as expected. But we had bought tickets on the promise of Jeff Beck appearing but in the event he pulled out with 'amplification problems'. Roy Orbison was just 'the guy with the big hit who's top of the bill' as far as we were concerned as the blues, rock, and psychedelic fans that we so

Poster for Small Faces, Moody Blues Concert
The Pavilion, Bournemouth on 19th June 1966
Courtesy of the Bourne Beat Bar, Bournemouth

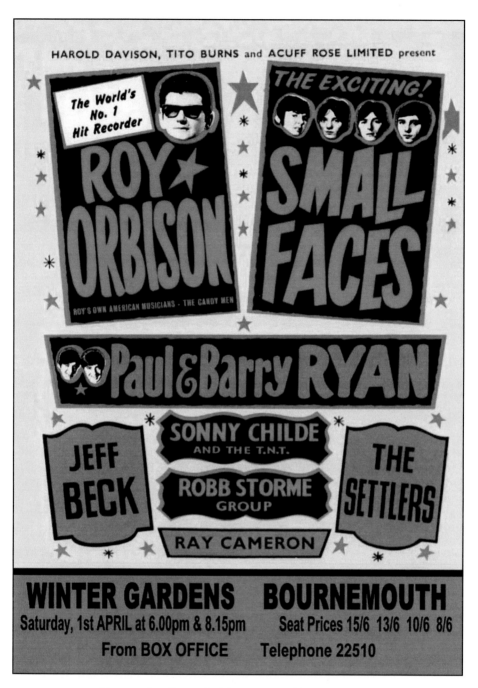

**Poster for Roy Orbison, Small Faces Concert
The Winter Gardens, Bournemouth on 1st April 1967**
Courtesy of the Bourne Beat Bar, Bournemouth

staunchly were and we would suffer him just to get our money's worth. At the time, this was just outright musical snobbery on our part as it wouldn't have been 'hip' to have admitted we had enjoyed his music, even if we had. If anything, we probably thought he was riding the wave of his No.1 record and would probably fizzle out like the proverbial and pun-like 'Shooting Star', whereas instead, as we now know, he hung around to become an International Superstar whom we would enjoy and respect in his own right. Roy's music, to these ears 40 years on anyway, was definitely waving the Rock 'n' Roll banner, but our judgment at the time was stupidly biased, simply for the sake of the then current fashion and trends.

So we had bought the tickets to see Jeff Beck, and guitar god that he was even then, it was worth it, but our disappointment at not only his pathetic excuse at jumping off the tour but also that we had been miserably let down by him would be short-lived, as Beck's replacement on the bill was announced to be…

The Creation.

Before Jimmy Page began impressing Led Zeppelin audiences by playing his guitar with a violin bow, The Creation's guitarist, Eddie Phillips, had already done so on the band's first two singles, released on the somewhat obscure Planet Records label in 1966. *Making Time* came out in June and *Painter Man* in the October (it went into the Top 40 and was later covered as a disco version by Boney M). The B-sides to those two groundbreaking singles were *Try And Stop Me* and *Biff, Bang, Pow* and they were equally as good as their A-side counterparts, yet somehow The Creation, to my mind anyway, could never match up the remainder of their catalogue with those four amazing songs. Those tracks were up there alongside the magnificence of The Who, The Yardbirds and the best of them, but cover versions of *Hey Joe* and *All Along The Watchtower* along with other weaker songs like *If I Stay Too Long*, *Cool Jerk* and *Girls Are Naked* being average pop fodder, the tracks just weren't in the same league.

Luckily, a visit to 'You Tube' on the Internet will find The Creation playing the two A-sides on the *Beat Club* mid-60s TV pop programme, which was the German equivalent of our own *Top of the Pops*.

The Creation were regarded, much like The Who at the time, as a Mod/Psychedelic/Flower Power Pop band, though after *Making Time* and *Painter Man* the band did not capitalise on their success in the UK. However, they continued doing well around Europe, especially in Germany where they went on to release LPs and more singles but then split up. However, with Rock 'n' Roll still bubbling in their blood, The Creation reformed in the 1980s, and in 1995 recorded a gig for later DVD release under the title of *Red With Purple Flashes*, which is how they described their music. Although we appreciated seeing them at the time, and their appearance on the bill 'saved the evening for us Progressive/Psychedelic Rock snobs', with the benefit of hindsight, we were very fortunate to see them on a Bournemouth stage at the height of their fame.

*RIP Lead vocalist, Kenney Pickett (1942-1996), who also co-wrote Clive Dunn's *Granddad* No.1 hit.

The Who & The Troggs.

In 1966, our school, Lytchett Minster Secondary Modern, organised a trip for 25 of our form to go to Redlands College in Bristol to be 'guinea pigs' for half a dozen trainee teachers for *three weeks!* This was quite a groundbreaking thing to do at the time, and we went after all too numerous 'fund raisers' by the school and the Parent Teacher Association to buy it, in the school bus. It was a bit of a rickety old thing and our form master and mathematics teacher, Mr. Trickey, drove us there. Two or three of our fellow 15 year old class mates had brought along radios and we listened to the latest and, or so the media had told us, 'very suggestive' No.1 record *Wild Thing* by The Troggs. Although some younger readers might find it crazy to even consider that *Wild Thing* was or could be regarded as suggestive, well, you'd have to consider the lyrics with regard to the rather staid ethos that prevailed then into which we were born and brought up to appreciate it.

Although it did happen and children were often conceived 'on the wrong side of the sheets', as an accidental pregnancy would be described, the very idea of sex of any kind before marriage was severely frowned upon by our elders. The world then was very much of the 'old fuddy-duddy' mentality which is superbly illustrated in Agatha Christie's *Miss Marple* TV shows starring Joan Hickson, so as a consequence our generation was brought up with very strong values concerning sex and relationships with females. Of course, behind the facade that we built for our parents' benefit, we were just as keen to have relationships with the females as they were with us and it must also be borne in mind that we were still within the 'St. Trinians' era of the girls wearing stockings and suspenders to school. Tights (or pantyhose, as is their 'Americanism') had not long been invented and would only become mass-produced cheaply enough to be bought and worn about 6 months later. This was quite useful as in turn the mini skirt could not have achieved its height (excuse the pun!) of fashion without this invention.

So we had been taught to keep our hands to ourselves and that sex before marriage was forbidden fruit, but with 13 boys and 12 girls away from home in Bristol at an extremely hormonal 15 years of age, well, I rest my case. So you can perhaps understand how *Wild Thing was* considered rather suggestive and naughty in its day and we were even surprised when we were not told to switch off the radios when the song was playing, but perhaps the teachers hadn't caught on just yet?

They had planned all sorts of things for us to do on this trip such as visits to several different types of factories (Robinson's Wax Paper and Fry's Chocolates amongst them), a visit to one of the then 'new' comprehensive schools and an evening at the opera. Visiting the comprehensive school was the funniest as us lads had what we considered to be 'long hair' but when we walked into the hall at this school one of the students who, like all of his contemporaries, had hair down past his shoulder-blades asked, "Haven't any of you lot got long hair yet, then?" We felt quite offended because we thought our locks were rather risqué and 'long' at that time.

They had some 'do' or another going on one evening, something we considered boring like opera and the attendance was optional. Well, someone had noticed a poster advertising The Who playing Bristol's Corn Exchange on the same evening as the opera: May 11th 1966. So as soon as the word spread about The Who gig, virtually everyone turned down the opera and as we could go 'out on the town' on such an occasion if we so wished, we thought about trying to find the Corn Exchange. After so many of us turned down the opera event, our teachers quickly caught on to the fact we were hoping to discreetly go along to see The Who instead. So, Mr. Trickey called the boys together in the boys' sleeping quarters situated in a large hall where each of us had a single bed and a locker, almost Forces style, to announce that as virtually everyone had opted *not* to go to the opera, we were grounded for the evening. Miss. Ryder, the headmistress, did the same with the girls. This was devastating news for most of us, and Trickey asked if anyone would like to reconsider their decision about going along to the opera? Quite a few did but some of us lads who had been really annoyed at this action decided to stick to our guns and stay grounded. It was worthwhile anyway as Kevin and Pete, although un-amplified, played through some of the songs they knew, and tried explaining the chords for The Who's *Substitute*, which only went further in strengthening my adoration, if not the resolve to learn to play the guitar.

However, despite having The Who's gig blown out from beneath our feet, we would not be completely cheated out of our glory in seeing a pop or rock band 'live and in-the-flesh'. On May 22nd, 1966, a trip had been organised for a visit to Cheddar Caves, in Somerset. We had already been camping in the Forest of Dean and experienced a midnight hike, which at the time was believed to have been *the* high point of the whole trip. It definitely had been for me being a youthful and keen *Daily Telegraph* 'Sky at Night' map back-garden stargazer when we had all lain down in the middle of a gravel track for 10 minutes looking up at an absolutely perfect Milky Way and also one of the girls had given me the first real 'snog' of my life. So what else was there better? Well, nothing, until this came along…

So, off we went to Cheddar Caves in the old school bus. In my younger day I was hopeless at travelling, especially in buses and coaches and tended to be sick at every opportunity. In fact, I was standing up getting some fresh air from the tiny, slide-open coach window, desperately trying to fend off the current bout of nausea, when someone said, "We're here!"

Bearing in mind I used to get sick on the 3 mile journey from home to Poole, then sick again on the trip back, I had done well at not only getting from Lytchett Minster to Bristol but also in going on these numerous outings. Indeed, such was my fear of this travel sickness I deliberately fluffed my 11+ Exams to avoid travelling the 5 or 6 miles to Wimborne Grammar School every day on their old coach.

Cycling to Lytchett Manor was just the job for a travel sick urchin like me and Wimborne Grammar seemed to be very much how we imagined life in the *Tom Brown's Schooldays* and the *Billy Bunter* stories and they did far too much sport for my liking. I mean, I still don't even know the rules of a football match now, let alone then, and I managed to get banned from ever playing football at the Manor.

The ban, funnily enough, was a far from a punishment. Running around a football field with a load of lads was not my ideal. Cross country running, which I plumped for, brought with it female company. Unless it was an actual inter-school or inter-house race, we would run until we were out of sight of the school, and then spend an hour and a half just ambling around the course chatting to any of the girls who happened to have come along. This was far better than being with a team of boys playing football as far as I was concerned. Usually, someone had a packet of cigarettes. The school hard-nuts and never-do-wells would also willingly go for X-country rather than running around a football pitch, too, so it was also another rebel stance in smoking with the school tough-nuts. If we didn't take part in PE or games, we would be whacked with either a plimsoll or the cane, unless we had a doctor's certificate, so we chose any other option just to avoid a beating and X-country running was about the best on offer given the circumstances.

But here we were at Cheddar.

Thank goodness for that!

We ambled out of the bus and began our tour around Cheddar Caves with the guide talking us through everything there was to see. We were expected to take notes, as we were supposed to write a diary to tell the school governors and our parents what a wonderfully educational and worthwhile time we'd had at Redlands, when the guide made the biggest mistake of all time when he said, "We will have to stop here and wait for a few minutes, as there's a pop group having their picture taken just ahead of us." I bet he rued the day he said 'pop group', but too late, the words had been spoken and all 25 of us didn't give a fig about Cheddar Caves any more. The guide and our teachers, much as they tried to stop us and dished out all sorts of nasty verbal penances of what we would suffer if we didn't stay put, failed miserably and quickly realised that:

Pop group + teenagers = complete bedlam!

On our day trip to Cheddar Caves we had stumbled across none other than The Troggs! They were having the album cover photo taken for their first LP, *From Nowhere The Troggs*, and as Troglodytes were cave dwellers, this was how and why the photo session inside Cheddar Caves was taking place. Luckily, girls carry note books and some even had autograph books and despite the fact we should have had something for making our diary notes, we had to beg the girls for a scrap of paper to get The Troggs autographs; sometimes, making promises we knew we couldn't keep just to get one precious sheet.

Chris Britton, guitarist with The Troggs

Between us, I think we managed to get perhaps 3 black and white photos of The Troggs signing autographs and found it funny when singer, Reg Presley, which was how we knew him, asked drummer,

Ronnie Bond, what his name actually was. Born Reginald Maurice Ball, he had changed his surname to Presley to make it sound more fitting for the pop world, but had forgotten it already. Mind you, *Wild Thing* had taken off rather quickly and Reg, who was a bricklayer by trade, is known to have said in an interview, "We were working up on the scaffolding and they played *Wild Thing* on the radio and the DJ said it was the new No.1! I threw down my trowel and told the boys to share out my tools. I knew I wouldn't be going back to the building site again!"

Ronnie Bond, drummer with The Troggs at Cheddar Caves, 1966
Photo session for their *From Nowhere The Troggs* Album

So we were immediate Troggs fans and the band sold 25 more copies of *From Nowhere The Troggs* on the strength of meeting us on our now abandoned trip to Cheddar Caves. Our teachers and the students must have put the experience down to 'high-jinx' as no retribution was exacted after we had ignored their commands to "stay put and not leave the party to go a see this pop group!"

Funnily enough, on our last evening at Redlands, the college threw a party for us and the students for whom we had been the guinea pigs happened to have a band of their own and played a couple of sets during the party, which was an excellent ending for the trip.

In essence, our visit had been to find out if every time a group of people got together, would it turn into William Golding's *Lord of The Flies* situation? And it had, much to everyone's disappointment, including ours. But we had enjoyed it and had a lot of fun despite this and every one of us had grown up and learned a lot of different things, mainly about the opposite sex, and how to, or indeed how not to get on with them.

It had also been 3 weeks away from home, which for me, as my father was still rather strict, had been absolute heaven and in many ways I regretted the ride home. We had been treated as adults for the first time in our lives by people not that much older than ourselves, and that had meant a great deal. Being caught out in our 'Escape From Redlands College' to go and see The Who had been a learning curve in knowing who to trust and who not to, as one or more of 'the babies' of the class, who were not enjoying life away from Mummy and Daddy and hence didn't want to be a part of it, had let the cat out of the bag deliberately to ruin our attempt. Even now, though, I feel sure Eric, Kevin, Pete and I would have made it to see The Who had our plans not been thwarted but I don't think any of the others had enough Rock 'n' Roll in them at the time to take the chance of leaving the safety of the college to traipse the streets of Bristol trying to find the Corn Exchange. Yet the four of us *would have completed our mission!* At the time, The Who meant the whole world to me and I was probably the most disappointed.

Many years later, probably in the late 1980s, at a Troggs gig at The White Buck Inn at Burley in the New Forest, Eric and I spent half an hour or so at the bar talking to the band. (By this time, Pete Staples, the original Troggs bass player had left the band, and the line-up was: Reg Presley (vocals), Chris Britton (guitar), Ronnie Bond (drums [1940-1992]) and Tony Murray (bass). Whilst the rest of the crowd who had come along to see them were younger, they didn't realise that four of the six 'old farts' at the bar were The Troggs. So we enjoyed this comparative freedom by asking the band a few questions we'd had bursting inside us for twenty odd years. Of course, after they had played their set we couldn't get near them for new fans, as those people had now realized they were the band, but we'd enjoyed our 'quality time' with them earlier when nobody but us knew who they were.

I mentioned the Cheddar Caves photo session to Reg Presley on that occasion and he couldn't believe it, as he said, "Do you know what? I was only thinking about that last week and now you two turn up and tell us you were there! That is the strangest thing!" We also told Reg that after seeing him smoke 'Embassy' cigarettes at Cheddar Caves we made sure we smoked 'Embassy' as well; to which he remarked "But I don't ever remember smoking 'Embassy' in my life, it must have been all I could get hold of at the time; they were probably bought out of desperation from a cigarette machine!"

Poster for The Who Concert
The Pavilion, Bournemouth on 2nd April 1969
Courtesy of the Bourne Beat Bar, Bournemouth

The Jimi Hendrix Experience.

The younger generation may not understand why Jimi Hendrix was such a phenomenon. To fully understand the effect he had on the music scene and its history, you would have to go back in time to September 1966 when he made his debut *Top of the Pops* appearance and listen to contemporary music for comparison. Jimi had been the rave of the London clubs since ex-Animals bassist and now his Manager, Chas Chandler, had brought him to the UK. The music press had reports about our guitar gods, Eric Clapton, Jeff Beck and The Who's Pete Townshend, going to see him play at The Revolution Club or The Bag O' Nails in London and being completely bowled over by his playing. In fact, one report mentioned someone (Eric Clapton, perhaps?) walking into one such club, and meeting with Jeff Beck coming out before the show had ended and asking, "Is he *that bad*, Jeff?" and Beck replying, "No, he's *that good!*"

Jimi Hendrix literally took my breath away on *Top of the Pops* playing *Hey Joe*, and his name was on everyone's lips at school next day. Being Friday, it was Rural Science, and the day we were always the *Top of the Pops* and the music scene's most would-be pundits.

Up until that point, every other guitarist had looked upon the element of his instrument feeding back to the amplifier as a curse, and did their best to eliminate it but Jimi Hendrix used it to his advantage. Even his roadie (Eric Barrett) couldn't set-up and tune his instrument, apparently, as he played it with *everything* turned to the highest volume. He was a phenomenon and *we will never* see such genius again!

Many years later, in 2005, I would see The Hamsters playing live at the local Mr. Kyps venue. They play Jimi Hendrix and ZZ Top music - exceptionally well. Standing in the middle of the venue about halfway back between the stage and the sound-desk, The Hamsters played a couple of Hendrix songs and I must say they were as close as anyone has ever been to 'the real Jimi'! A couple of guys there to enjoy the evening were standing close by, and during the break between songs one said to the other, "It's a bit loud, isn't it!" His friend nodded and frowned. I leaned across and said, "If he wasn't loud, he (the Hamster's guitarist only known as 'Slim') wouldn't be able to play Jimi Hendrix music as well as he does!"

Hendrix' essence, other than being an astonishing guitar genius, was based on his use of controlled volume and feedback and the ability to do so with apparent ease. Watch him on any video or DVD, he's just effortlessly enjoying what he's doing and at the start of his 'Woodstock' performance *even he* isn't quite Jimi Hendrix until he walks back to turn everything up to *full volume* and then he is indeed, Jimi Hendrix we know and love! The amazing thing was, though, we managed to see him live on stage and I will always be grateful for that privilege, although at the time we didn't know his career would only last for just 4 short years.

The Walker Brothers, Cat Stevens, Jimi Hendrix & Engelbert Humperdinck.

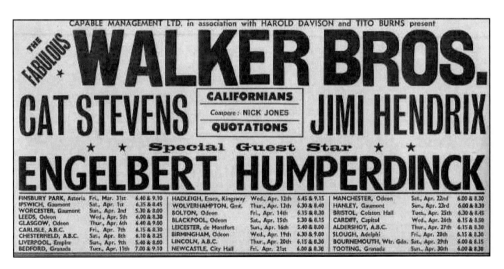

This 1967 package tour was a bit of a strange for the simple reason The Walker Brothers fans were our peers as teenage girls, Cat Stevens was a Pop Chart act, Engelbert Humperdinck appealed to those teenage girls' Mums and Jimi Hendrix was about as out-and-out psychedelic rock as you could get. However, the one thing they all had in common was their presence in the UK national singles and albums charts at the time, so it had something for everyone; bizarre as it perhaps may seem today.

The Walker Brothers had huge hits with *The Sun Ain't Gonna Shine Any More, Make It Easy On Yourself* and *My Ship Is Coming In* amongst many more and again, as an example of their popularity to younger readers, they would be about as big as U2!

Engelbert Humperdinck, who is still playing shows in Las Vegas today, had massive No.1 hits with *Release Me* and *The Last Waltz* and was, as mentioned before, very much a Mum's favourite.

Cat Stevens was touting his very first hits with *I Love My Dog, Matthew & Son* and *I'm Gonna Get Me A Gun*, long before he reinvented himself and moved into the realms of even bigger mega-stardom with *Moon Shadow* and *Morning Has Broken*.

Jimi Hendrix, of course, was for me the ultimate and that's not just a retrospective outburst of sorrow reflecting upon his untimely death. Jimi Hendrix was the best guitarist of all time and always will be, and guitars, especially guitars played loud and with feedback were and still are just my thing, so from that moment on *Top of the Pops* when I first saw him, he was my ultimate idol for many years.

Much like the trend that was prevalent when The Rolling Stones toured in 1964, this tour would also play 2 houses per day, an early and a late. This was customary to allow those who lived further away to attend the early performance and thus give them sufficient time to get either their bus or train back at a reasonable hour, as not many people owned cars at this time. Those who lived closer, of course, would attend the second house, as public transport ended at 9.30pm, so there was still time to get home.

Getting a bus from one such 'late show' with cousin, Richard, we somehow managed to board the wrong one, ending up in Wallisdown which, if you lived in Upton as we did was completely the wrong direction. Fortunately, the bus was returning to Poole Bus Station and we explained to the bus conductor that we didn't have enough money for the return fare. So he kindly 'turned a blind eye' to our presence on the bus but told us if an Inspector got on we'd be kicked off and would have to walk.

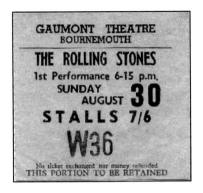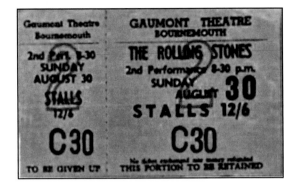

Tickets for the Rolling Stones concert at The Gaumont, Bournemouth
2 performances on 30th August 1964

We were getting a bit worried at this predicament but tended, as we did in those days, to look upon this as something of an adventure (as the camaraderie from the two wars when everyone got along and helped one another out was still with us). Luckily, no Inspector boarded the bus, so we arrived back the bus station, thanked the conductor and began walking along Poole High Street in the direction of home.

At the time it was possible to drive up and down the High Street and it was also part of the bus route. Richard and I had just about reached Woolworths, wishing we had 1/6d (7½ pence, today!) to get fish and chips from The Amity chip shop opposite as we were starving, when a 'Black Maria' pulled up alongside us. One of the 'coppers' inside asked what we were doing wandering around at such a late hour, about 11pm! We told our story and they were sympathetic and offered us a lift home in the van. This was great, because we arrived home at about the same time we would have done so had we caught *the right bus* in the first place. But if our parents found out we had been brought home in a Black Mariah, then I dread to think of the penance we would have suffered.

Probably, we would have been banned from going to any more concerts, so we kept quiet about getting on the wrong bus and hoped none of the neighbours saw us getting out of a police van! Luckily, no one did, but when you consider how free-and-easy youngsters today are with their parents and the police yet we were terrified of the consequences we might have had to face had our parents found out we had 'wasted police time being idiots and not paying attention to see where the bus was going!' The thing was, when we stepped on the bus, the sign told us it would be going to Poole, and it wasn't wrong, but it would get there via Wallisdown and it wasn't the trip our tickets had paid for, so this was the reason we became unstuck.

The Walker Brothers split up and almost faded away. Drummer, Gary Leeds, came back with Gary Leeds' Rain with little success, but Scott Walker still remains something of an icon, making albums and performing live infrequently.

The Biggest Pop Package Tour of all Time Plays The Winter Gardens!

On November 15th 1967, we went to see what would become regarded in later years as 'The Biggest Pop Package Tour Of All Time' when it played one night at Bournemouth Winter Gardens as part of a full UK tour with the still phenomenal bill featuring Jimi Hendrix, The Move, Pink Floyd, The Nice, Amen Corner, Outer Limits and Eire Apparent which would probably constitute a Festival today! This was also the tour when, as the archives of Rock legend now confirms, Lemmy Kilmister, who later found his own well deserved fame in Hawkwind and Motorhead, was one of the roadies for Jimi Hendrix (1942-1970). And it was quite some show, with Pink Floyd's groundbreaking psychedelia being an exceptional 'wow factor' of its day by projecting light through glass 'slides' filled with coloured oil onto the band as they played onstage. This might sound limp-wristed by today's light show extravaganzas but was rather exceptional at the time and after all, it had to start somewhere.

Much like most theatre and concert shows at the time, this one was no exception in having both an 'early' and a 'late' house with one at approximately 6.15pm and another at 8.45pm. So how did they fit so many bands into two hours? - with a revolving stage. Whilst one band played, the road crew would be setting up the next band behind a screen on the other half of the semi-circle. Eire Apparent would get about 10 minutes for their set, then the stage would be turned around 180 degrees and Outer Limits would play their 10 minutes. Amen Corner, being higher in the league, may have had 15 minutes, and so on, with Jimi Hendrix at the top of the bill being given a much more extravagant 40 minute set. The tour played 15 venues around the UK like this, with the first in London at The Royal Albert Hall.

Often I have been asked what it was like to have watched Jimi Hendrix playing live and, being the guitar freak that I always have been, I can only say that he was phenomenal. When asked what songs he played, I usually cite the *Live At Monterey* DVD as roughly the set list he might have used: (*Killing Floor / Foxy Lady / Like A*

Rolling Stone / Rock Me Baby / Hey Joe / The Wind Cries Mary / Purple Haze / Wild Thing), as the Monterey gig had been played on June 19th 1967 and there we were watching him on November 15th. But the *Are You Experienced?* LP had been released in the August, so he may have mixed and matched some of the Monterey songs, perhaps, with live favourites from that album, like *I Don't Live Today, Love Or Confusion, Red House* or *Can You See Me?* No, Jimi didn't set fire to or smash his guitar in Bournemouth but we heard that was wearing his boots that night as he'd played barefoot the gig before and had cut his foot on an effects pedal.

And it was and would be quite something to be fortunate enough, if only by way of our age and the fact that we had bought the tickets, that we were able to see Jimi Hendrix in concert, as little did anyone know or even imagine at the time that he would only have another 3 years to live.

These shows took place in 1967, yet today, some younger fans still find it difficult to believe such a tour with so many major names on the bill actually took place. But those bands had just started off at the time: Pink Floyd had moved up to the second division and were plugging their *Arnold Layne* and *See Emily Play* hit singles, and also their first album with the *Wind In The Willows* inspired title of *The Piper At The Gates Of Dawn*. Jimi Hendrix had *Hey Joe, Purple Haze* and *The Wind Cries Mary* singles whilst also promoting his *Are You Experienced?* first LP. The Move would have been pushing their excellent *Night of Fear, I Can Hear The Grass Grow* and *Flowers In The Rain* pop singles, and no doubt their blandly titled *The Move* first LP. Irish rockers, Eire Apparent, had signed to both Hendrix' manager Chas Chandler and also the then newly-formed Track Records label. Hendrix went on to produce and play on the Eire Apparent *Sunrise* LP but after achieving little success, the band later split with some members re-forming into The Grease Band (who then backed Joe Cocker) with guitarist Henry McCulloch, being the mainstay throughout.

42

The Troggs (again!) & Gene Pitney.

The Troggs headlined another tour of the UK with 'one hit wonder' David Garrick who had roused a little female interest after a fairly insipid minor hit titled *Dear Mrs. Appleby*. Australian band by the name of Normie Rowe and the Playboys played their own set and then backed the 'Tour Special Guest' Gene Pitney. In an effort to shift them from division 3 into division 2 (but it didn't work as they had nothing strikingly original on offer), was an up-and-coming band who were also on The Troggs' Page One Records label called The Loot.

This gig took place on March 17th 1967 at The Winter Gardens. Eric and I took my brother's single lens reflex camera and had it hanging around my neck under a bulky jacket. Security was strict, of course, as The Winter Gardens staff and bouncers still didn't quite know how to handle these 'new-fangled pop groups' and the crowds of screaming fans they attracted.

Troggs Concert, Winter Gardens Bournemouth, 1967

Eric and I had seats along the left hand side wall, but had to stand to see properly. When 'the coast was clear' and neither of us could see any bouncers, I'd take a quick couple of photos, and Eric would give me a nudge if any bouncers appeared to enable me to tuck the camera away and not get caught. Being an SLR camera which needed manual focusing, this may be the reason why the shots are slightly blurred; flash was not used, either, so this may be why they are a bit 'grainy'. Nevertheless, like the Cheddar Caves Troggs photos, they are rare shots and this is their first ever publication.

In the photos, you can see the 'cattle bars' to keep the screaming fans back in place. One of the pictures has singer, Reg Presley, on bass, with usual bassist, Pete Staples, on tambourine and vocals for the bands cover version of Bo Diddley's song *Mona*. Pete also sang the song on the *Trogglodynamite* album.

Troggs Concert, Winter Gardens Bournemouth, 1967

Dave Dee, Dozy, Beaky, Mick & Tich.

Also on the tour mentioned above, they were a band from nearby Salisbury and much like The Troggs they were continually in the charts with Top Ten or No.1 hits like *Hold Tight, Hideaway, The Legend Of Xanadu, Bend It, Okay* and *Zabadak*.

It was great having so many stars on one bill, and to be able to enjoy memorable package tours like this at The Winter Gardens was quite something, but as a sign of the times, those metal barriers had been installed to stop over-excited female fans getting onstage. The Beatles and The Rolling Stones had unwittingly created a huge problem with their fans ripping their clothes and pulling out their hair for souvenirs and almost every other band at the time suffered the same fate, or would it be glory?

The Troggs and Dave Dee (David Harman [1941-2009]), Dozy,

Beaky, Mick & Tich had a few more hits before going on in later years to play the 60s circuit of pubs and clubs in the UK and Europe, and also Butlins 60s Festivals. Troggs' singer and main songwriter, Reg Presley, however, would make a few £million when the 1980s pop band called Wet, Wet, Wet covered their *Love Is All Around* song, taking it to No.1 on the strength of its appearance in the *Four Weddings And A Funeral* film in 1994.

The Move.

All of these tours played Bournemouth's Winter Gardens but the town's Pavilion Theatre not only provided 'sit down performances' but also played host to 'standing' concerts in the Pavilion Ballroom, which was and still is located at an entrance to the right hand side of the venue with the ballroom situated over the top of the back-end of the theatre, so to speak.

The Move were a huge favourite at the time and had played to packed and enthusiastic crowds of local fans several times before at the Pavilion. Their July 5th 1968 show there would be no exception; the venue jam-packed with people shoulder-to-shoulder jostling for prime position at the front of the stage. Each time they played one of these shows three attractive young women would always be there. This being the height of the mini skirt era, they were dressed in what would become some of the atypical 'groupie' attire: skinny top, no bra and a mini skirt or dress so short parents and grandparents would regard them as 'indecent' or 'disgraceful' (but most males at the gig thought they were amazing!). Going by their looks it appeared as if they were identical twins who had brought along a like-minded friend. It was plain their intention was to get backstage with The Move and, of course, they would as they were regarded as 'the spoils' of being in a band and in many cases, groupies like these would be one of the main reasons why adolescent young men learned to play a guitar and wanted to be in a group in the first instance. (And who can blame them, what a fabulous ulterior motive.

Like footballer, Peter Crouch said recently when asked, "What would you have been if you hadn't been a footballer?" to which he smiled and replied, "A virgin!" And that anecdote would also apply to a great many rock musicians).

The Move always played an excellent set of not only their hits, but also some of the old Rock 'n' Roll standards and also a few covers of songs by their peers, like Spooky Tooth, Love and The Byrds. A superb band to see live, they released their *Something Else By The Move Live* 5-track EP, which was a massive favourite for their fans. It became a rarity during the vinyl years but was re-released as part of a Box Set Anthology during the 'noughties' along with the other songs recorded at The Marquee Club in London in 1968. The full set-list for the Marquee was: *Move Bolero / It'll Be Me / Too Much In Love / Flowers In The Rain / Fire Brigade / Stephanie Knows Who / Something Else / So You Want To Be A Rock 'n' Roll Star / The Price Of Love / Piece Of My Heart / (Your Love Keeps Lifting Me) Higher And Higher / Sunshine Help Me* and their Pavilion set would have been similar. The band at this time was Carl Wayne ([1943-2004] vocals), Roy Wood (guitar / vocals), Trevor Burton (guitar / vocals), Ace Kefford (bass) and Bev Bevan (drums / vocals).

Note: Up-and-coming bands may like to heed this piece of advice: make sure you give your groupie a neat spirit drink before kissing her as you never know how she had to favour a roadie as a means of getting to you!

The Who. (again!)

The Who would play The Pavilion Ballroom twice, once with local support band, Bram Stoker. As an ardent fan and proud member of The Who Fan Club with all their 45s and albums, going to see them live was a foregone conclusion as there would have been nothing in my life more important. They were superb. Even though I felt disappointed when Pete Townshend didn't smash his guitar, despite my standing in front of him at both shows waiting to catch the bits, they would be there, along with Hendrix and Cream, as my top 3 all time favourite bands up to and including 1970.

John Entwistle (1944-2002), of course, hardly moved at all as was his way, Roger Daltrey was the amazing singer he always has been, and Keith Moon (1946-1978) poured vodka over his snare and tom-tom drum skins at one point during the set when Pete Townshend was introducing a song so when he began playing the vodka splashed and looked like bullets hitting water. Moon (THE Loon), of course, thought it was hilarious.

They had recorded *Tommy* between late 1968 and March 1969, and then played The Pavilion Ballroom April 2nd 1969, and the general consensus of opinion from reviews on www.thewholive.de is that their set was very similar to the (fuller, re-issued) *Live At Leeds* album. But they returned on August 30th 1969, with the set consisting of: *Heaven And Hell / I Can't Explain / It's A Boy / 1921 / Amazing Journey / Sparks / The Hawker / Christmas / The Acid Queen / Pinball Wizard / Do You Think It's Alright? / Fiddle About / There's A Doctor / Go To The Mirror / Smash The Mirror / I'm Free / Tommy's Holiday Camp / We're Not Gonna Take It / Summertime Blues / Shakin' All Over / My Generation.*

The day after this gig The Who played The Isle of Wight Festival. Bournemouth was closer to the island than London, so prior to the short ferry-hop over to the festival they had used the Bournemouth date as a 'warm-up' for the higher profile show and had earned a gig fee into the bargain.

As big a Who fan as I was, and still am, *Tommy* didn't cut the mustard for me. Agreed, the concept was radical and ground-breaking but I found it boring to sit through the whole thing either on record or live but obviously I was in the minority as it shot The Who into the superstar status they have enjoyed ever since.

OK, *Pinball Wizard* is up there with their all-time greats and even though the rest of the pop world adored this Rock Opera, it wasn't the balls-to-the-wall thrashing and smashing Who I had grown to adore. *I Can See For Miles* is and always will be my all-time favourite Who track and I can only reiterate the headline the late Penny

Valentine (1943-2003) used in her review of the single in *Disc & Music Echo*, in that she thought it sounded 'Like Eight Express Trains Going Through A Tunnel At Once!' And yes, there have been far heavier tracks recorded and released since, but that vinyl single, played on a solid and sturdy old record player with red hot valves and solid-state circuitry from the 1967 era was an absolutely frightening and at the same time exhilarating experience and just about *the* 'heaviest' record on the planet. Yet today, on CD and through modern (micro-chipped) hi-fi equipment the track sounds rather diluted but with Pete Townshend himself citing *I Can See For Miles* as his favourite at 'capturing the true spirit of The Who in one 3 minute song', and 'To me, it was the ultimate Who record, yet it didn't sell, I spat on the British record buyer when it didn't get to No.1 in the Charts' you can see that I am not alone in adoring this superb Who track! (It achieved No.10 in the UK and No.9 in America, where it would be their biggest selling single.)

Note: A chap named Roger Airey was a work colleague a few years ago. Roger told me that he and his brother attended a Who gig in the 60s at Yeovil Town Hall, I believe. Townshend smashed his guitar there and Roger's brother managed to get the neck. He had it 'tucked in a corner of his bedroom for years, and then threw it away because he got fed up with looking at it'.

Bram Stoker.

They supported The Who at The Pavilion gig in August 1969, were Bournemouth based and impressive. Both the band's history and rock legend itself tells that The Who's Roger Daltrey was equally impressed by their set. So much so, he asked for contact details and later invited them to record some demos at his Berkshire home.

Bram Stoker had formed in the summer of 1969 by classically trained Hammond organist Tony Bronsdon, guitarist Pete Ballam, and drummer Rob Haines who then recruited bassist John Bavin; so their gig with The Who had been an early event in their career.

Pete and Rob had been working together in their own band for 2 years and found a kindred musical spirit in Tony. They were young, enthusiastic and inspired by the new 'progressive' music emerging from the rock scene at the time.

But in composing their own material and by experimentation with those new styles, Bram Stoker forged ahead in their own direction and, influenced by the Gothic image of the band's name, acquired their now famous 'Progressive Classical Rock / Gothic Rock' label.

They rehearsed in a disused night club in Poole before taking on any live gigs but that show with The Who would prove to be a pivotal point in their career.

A few months later, the demos they had made at Daltrey's home led to Bram Stoker being signed by one-time Rolling Stones co-manager, Tony Calder. This in turn led to the 1972 release of the *Heavy Rock Spectacular* LP on the Windmill Record label (WMD 117). Remembering their name from the set they played at The Pavilion show, I snapped up the album in Woolworths in Poole High Street for 19/11d.

Bram Stoker reformed in 2004 with original members Tony Bronsdon on Hammond organ and John Bavin on bass. They have been joined by Pat Flynn on guitar and Pete Rumble on drums. Their *Rock Paranoia* album was made available for download by Digimix

Records in September 2007. It consists of the *Heavy Rock Spectacular album tracks: Born To Be Free / Ants / Fast Decay / Blitz / Idiot / Fingal's Cave /Extensive Corrosion / Poltergeist* - plus the previously unreleased *Collusion Illusion / Scarborough Fair* from the same sessions.

More 'Pop' on TV!

By 1967, the TV media had realised 'pop music' wasn't going to go away. Top DJ of the era, Simon Dee, was given a talk show on which he would feature a guest band each week and during May '67, much to our delight, he featured The Kinks, Cream and The Troggs. Children's Friday teatime television show *Crackerjack* would also feature The Troggs amongst many others and a Granada ITV show by the name of *Rave* had featured The Move and Pink Floyd during March. This proved beyond all reasonable doubt that neither we nor our 'noisy pop music' was going to go away, and much as our elder and very disappointed generations would despise both us and 'those bloody long haired yobbos', they had to learn to live with us, which didn't sit gladly in most cases.

Setchfields Record Shop.

Always a keen record buyer, in Poole town itself, Poole Music Stores and Bourne Radio were at The George Hotel end of the High Street, with Setchfields at the 'Old Town' end near Poole Quay and The Antelope Hotel.

Terry Meads, whose parents owned Setchfields, had persuaded them to expand the newsagents and children's toys business into the record buying market which, as this new 'pop' phenomenon appeared to be taking off and staying with the younger generation, did so by opening a smaller shop next door. With great vats of records along each wall and free-standing racks as a centrepiece, one could spend hours flicking through the rafts of LPs. Setchfields also had 3 'listening booths' in which the customer could stand and hear a single or indeed a whole album before making up their mind to buy a copy or not.

Again, it was a sign of the times. If you appeared a reasonably polite and half-decent person and didn't overstep Terry's generosity, the best part of a couple of hours could be spent in Setchfields listening to an album or two in one of the booths with the necessary speakers installed to achieve and enjoy the 'full stereo effect'.

Sometimes, a friend would also drop in at the shop and share the booth for a while, listening to whatever record was playing, so it was quite a social thing unlike the sterile, shrink-wrapped/fitted with an anti-theft device/corporate world the high street record shop is today. In so many ways, and let's be honest all we had was vinyl and reel-to-reel tape, our world has now progressed but is it really progress? Like the scene described in Setchfields, it was a far better and friendlier world, and today, despite this so-called 'progress', we have lost that post-war camaraderie. The general public, and even the staff who serve in the shops are so hostile now, there seems to be very little friendliness amongst anyone, and it is such a pity that it takes a World War to encourage people to get along.

And whilst it is progress that the Internet age has brought us the best and biggest record shop in the world in Amazon and the younger generations can download their songs but in doing so, we are missing out on those social aspects of bumping into the like-minded music fans we used to meet when joyfully trudging from one local record shop to another. Such a pity! At that time, our record buying was confined to perhaps a 10 mile radius of our home town but today we can scour the record shops of the world on the Internet whilst sitting in a comfy seat!

But I digress.

The Jeff Beck Group with Rod Stewart & Ronny Wood.

The evening of November 3rd, 1967 would bring feelings of unsurpassed elation to the souls of school friends Eric and Kevin. Both of their families were keen *Evening Echo* readers and between them they had noticed an advert for The Jeff Beck Group, who would play The Poole Technical College Main Hall that evening.

Just prior to the flurry of most of us being old enough to take and pass our car driving tests, Eric went zooming off as the pillion passenger on Kevin's 'Lambretta' scooter, which he'd bought during our 5th year at school and had since 'modded it up' with mirrors, a fox tail and other assorted paraphernalia to see this once-in-a-lifetime gig, not that we knew it would be regarded as such at the time.

In fairness, owning a telephone was not common, so excuses can be made for not phoning through with the tip-off, but they could have dropped in on their way to the gig and advised that I cycle, hitch-hike, or do whatever it took to get there. But it was annoying at the time that they had just gone along to the gig without saying a word, leaving the rest of us to find out about it after the event.

Jeff Beck, of course, had been a hero of mine from his days with The Yardbirds on their *Roger The Engineer* 2nd LP and Kevin had always maintained a pre-knowledge about Rod Stewart and often declared that Rod Stewart was his uncle! This crazy statement had stemmed from Kevin seeing Stewart with Steam Packet when they supported The Rolling Stones at their Bournemouth Gaumont gig on July 18th, 1965. Rod had obviously been destined for his later stardom even then, as Kevin was impressed enough to quite regularly declare this madcap relationship with Rod Stewart long before everyone else really knew who he was. So with Eric as the biggest Yardbirds fan, (he had introduced us via his Five Live Yardbirds reel-to-reel tape), and Kevin this undying and very early name-dropping Rod Stewart fan; with the benefit of hindsight it was *the right thing to happen* when they managed to get to this gig and the rest of us didn't!

Beck had left The Yardbirds by then, of course, but The Jeff Beck Group, at the time they played Poole Tech, still had to record their first album, which would be titled *Truth*. Yet they included much of the material from that soon-to-be (1968) recorded and released album, like their own version of The Yardbirds *Shapes Of Things*, Tim Rose's *Morning Dew* and Willie Dixon's *I Ain't Superstitious* and *You Shook Me* just to get them well-rehearsed and ready for the studio.

The Jeff Beck Group were gigging virtually non-stop at this time in answer to the *three* hit singles Beck had under his belt in that same year, so a capacity crowd at every venue must have been guaranteed. Under the record production eagle eye of the then top pop svengali / hit guru, Mickie Most, (Michael Peter Hayes 1938-2003), Beck had almost begrudgingly racked up the evergreen 'DJs favourite' and played-at-every-party-in-the-world hit single, *Hi-Ho Silver Lining* and then, a couple of months later had followed it with *Tallyman*, both of which featured Jeff singing, which was something he detested doing. After those two 45s came the instrumental and almost Shadow's-like *Love Is Blue* single, which Vicky Leandros had sung as the Luxembourg entry for the 1967 Eurovision Song Contest.

Although Beck had recorded those three singles with Mickie Most, and in fairness, as such they had moved his name away from murky netherworld of hard-core Yardbirds' fans like us and into the public eye and consciousness. Jeff simply hated them vehemently, well, the A-sides at least.

But whether he liked them or not, they were out there and high in the National Top 40 Charts, yet the songs on the flip-sides of those Columbia Records 45s would be proudly played live alongside any of the other material, with *I've Been Drinking Again* (the B-side of *Love Is Blue*), and *Rock My Plimsoul* (spelled that way! The B-side of *Tallyman*), both of which feature Rod Stewart on vocals. The B-side of *Hi-Ho Silver Lining* was the incredible track titled *Beck's Bolero* and is based upon Maurice Ravel's classical piece, *Bolero*, and that studio recording featured Jeff Beck on guitar, Jimmy Page (then still working as Beck's replacement with The Yardbirds, then later with Led Zeppelin) also on guitar, The Who's Keith Moon on drums, session pianist (but who would later be a member of Beck's band, and then play on studio sessions with The Rolling Stones) Nicky Hopkins and (yet-to-be Led Zeppelin's) John Paul Jones, on bass. (There is a live version of this track on *You Tube*, played by Jeff Beck with his current band, recorded in the 'Noughties').

Following on from the success of those three Chart singles and the momentum they created in the public eye, anyone who played the A-sides but ignored the B-sides would have been just as surprised to have found those A-sides were also missing from the two albums, and how completely different they were to the blues and rock of the tracks included on them. With Jeff on guitar, Rod Stewart on vocals, Ronnie Wood (later with The Faces and The Rolling Stones) on bass and Micky Waller on drums and released in 1968 and 1969 respectively as *Truth* and *Beck-Ola*, they were quite stunning LPs for rock fans. Having some music by Jeff Beck from beyond The Yardbirds was quite amazing and unbeknown to anyone how Rod Stewart's career would take off in a couple of years time, the whole scene for The Jeff Beck Group seemed nice and rosy. But as ever, progress moves some of the music scene's golden moments onward, but thankfully, most are recorded for posterity, so they are never truly 'lost'.

Both of those albums have been prestigiously re-released on CD *with* those excellent B-sides included as bonus tracks along with the three A-sides, much to Jeff's disappointment, no doubt. Jeff seems to be one of those people who hate hearing their own voice and even today, in concert and in the live auditorium, he barely speaks from the beginning through to the end of the gig. It's the way he is and that's the way he runs his shows and you either like it or lump it.

Jeff continues to make usually instrumental albums to this day and performs live as mentioned above. Ronnie Wood has played guitar with The Rolling Stones since 1975 and Kevin's 'Uncle' Rod Stewart is the stadium superstar and multi-million selling album vocalist he became after his *Maggie May* single and *Every Picture Tells A Story* LP hits.

Just as a note out of interest, despite Jeff's publicly declared hatred for *Hi-Ho Silver Lining* (I don't think he'd tear up the Royalty cheque, though) and swearing he would never sing or play it again live, he relented for (ex-Small Faces bassist) Ronnie Lane's (1946-1997) ARMS Multiple Sclerosis Charity fund raising gig at The Royal Albert Hall in 1983 when he did so 'just for Ronnie', and appeared on the video of the show doing just that. Jeff also played part of the song on one of Jools Holland's shows. (Many other stars also played at this charity gig for Ronnie Lane: Eric Clapton, Steve Winwood, Bill Wyman and Charlie Watts all appeared and others joined in to play a similar gig for the charity in America).

The Dictators / Infantes Jubilate.

One Saturday morning in October 1968, four young men in their early twenties walked into Setchfields record shop in the Old Town of Poole High Street. Terry Meads welcomed them, and then approached me. "These lads are a local band from Wimborne, they're called Infantes Jubilate and we're doing a promo launch for *The Evening Echo* as they've just released a single and as a regular customer would you like to hang around and be in the photo with them?"

Of course, I agreed and why ever not? A local band who had released a single and on the Music Factory label (a division of MGM Records) no less! This was quite something! Until that time, I thought bands had to go to London and play the scene there to get noticed *and then* bag a recording contract to have a single or album released. But it seemed that Infantes Jubilate, whom, in fairness, I had never heard of before even though they were local, had bucked the system and cracked it! This surprised me, as most people in our age group were familiar with the majority of the bands on the local circuit, so these lads were unique! But most of all, it proved how ordinary people from close to where we lived *could* release records and be somewhat famous.

The A-side of the single being launched in Setchfields was titled *Exploding Galaxy* with *Take It Slow* on the flip, and the catalogue number was CUB 5. The *Echo* photographer arrived and took several pictures, (I think Terry also sneaked into it, and managed to grab one or two more people to flesh out the 'surrounding fans'), and one photo appeared in either *The Evening Echo* or *The Poole & Dorset Herald*, along with some blurb a few days later. But even though I bought a copy, that was about it for Infantes Jubilate. However, the decades have been extremely kind to them, and the A-side has cropped up on quite a few 'psychedelic '60s' compilation albums, initially, as a double vinyl LP, and more recently (2007) on the 10 CD box set titled *The Rubble Collection Volumes 11 to 20*.

INFANTES JUBILATE

Issued on the MGM spin-off label, Music Factory, "Exploding Galaxy" was promoted with an advert which featured a picture of this well-groomed and surprisingly ordinary-looking four-piece, and described their single as an "astronomical record". Colourful and unusual it certainly is — sounding like Patrick Campbell Lyons' Nirvana and incorporating a passage from a Beethoven symphony — though it is less accessible than many other 'odd' singles from this period. Its principal appeal lies in its excessive use of phasing; after the intro, the remainder of the record is swamped in this particularly effective studio gimmick.

● The 1965 Echo caption to this picture is hilarious: 'After seeing so many groups who appear to think one of the attributes which will get them in the top 10 is to have ultra-long, often greasy-looking hair styles, it is refreshing to note that a local group – The Dictators – favour short, neat and manly hairstyles. They have regular appointments with a Poole man's hairdresser and their good example could well be followed by all long-haired youths one still, unfortunately, sees around'. Has anyone got a picture of the lads today?

But the story behind the release of this single was a mixture of both pleasure and pain. The band had been on the gigging circuit, locally, nationally and in Europe, since 1962 under the name of The Dictators, and had released a couple of singles. Playing a gig at the Bournemouth Ice Rink in Westover Road, they were approached by a man who introduced himself as Jonathan Werne, who asked if they would like to record a single? The Dictators line up was Keith Pearce (lead guitar and lead vocals), Terry Avery (drums), Bob (Tony) Foster (bass guitar) and Dave Longley (rhythm guitar); and with the promise of brighter lights and bigger cities than they had seen before, and name-drops like *Top of the Pops*, they grabbed the opportunity with both hands. The only other thing they had to agree on was a name change for the band.

In a London recording studio, the band, now heralding their new name of Infantes Jubilate, *(Latin: joyful youth),* as chosen by Werne, along with composer, James Stevens and a 40-piece orchestra, recorded the *Exploding Galaxy* track; the orchestration of which had been based on Beethoven's 5th Symphony.

Werne had put the band into a plush hotel, given them a manicure, bought them tailor-made suits to wear onstage and also the latest brand new amps and a PA system; so life was looking great!

The single was released to become *Record Mirror's* 'Record of the Week' yet in *Disc & Music Echo,* reviewer Anne Nightingale thought it was 'pretentious'.

Back in Bournemouth and rehearsing one day, there was a knock on the door. It was composer, James Stephens. He looked as white as a sheet and scared stiff and told the band Werne had been a complete conman and his cheques had bounced all around London: for their hotel, hiring the orchestra, the suits, everything and could they please return the amps and PA otherwise he would end up buried in the Chiswick flyover! Worried at the threats, the band did as they were asked.

Within their short time as Infantes Jubilate, they had also left their local booking agency and signed, at Werne's insistence, to a London agent who, after the charade with the bounced cheques, didn't bother finding them any work. So, although none the worse for wear, the band had learnt a great deal from this sweet and sour experience, and bitterly disappointed, they quit the music business.

The Bee Gees played The Ritz when they first arrived in the UK from Australia in 1966/1967, and The Dictators were their support band.

At the time, *The Echo* printed both Bournemouth and Poole editions of the newspaper. A write-up and photo from the Setchfields record launch appeared in the 'Poole Edition' of *The Evening Echo* a few days later, but any copies have disappeared over the years, and the Poole edition of the newspaper has never been archived at any of the resource centres.

Keith Pearce: Today, an Internet Search for James Stevens has entries connected to The Churchill Society of London and mentions, along with his classical compositions, TV and film scores, *Exploding Galaxy*, claiming it reached No.1 in the Charts. How life would have been different if that was true.

THE DICTATORS

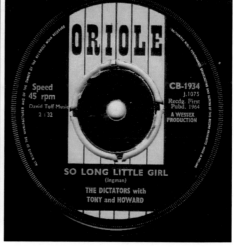

Brother's Bung.

Supporting The Alan Bown and Lemon Peel at the Pavilion Ballroom on August 30th 1968, Brother's Bung were the first band I remember covering just one artiste's repertoire. Plenty of other bands covered an across-the-board mixture of different band's music, but Brother's Bung were at the time the first to exclusively cover Jimi Hendrix' songs.

Conversely to the Jimi Hendrix Experience, however, Brother's Bung had an Afro-Caribbean bassist / lead singer, with their guitarist replicating the Hendrix sound and the drummer doing Mitch Mitchell's (1946-2008) bit, of course. They were quite something to see and hear, showstoppers in fact, as their audiences had never before watched a band playing a whole set of just one artiste's songs. So they were very unusual and deserved far more than support slots, I mean, to be billed below Lemon Peel? Who were they? No one remembers, but a good many will remember Brother's Bung as they were frequently on the support band circuit, and playing Hendrix songs brought them a great deal of fans and popularity!

Peter Green's Fleetwood Mac.

1969 would be something of a busy year, with Peter Green's Fleetwood Mac kicking it off with a gig at The Ritz on February 25th. The line-up playing would be: Peter Green (guitar and vocals), Jeremy Spencer (guitar and vocals) Danny Kirwan (guitar) Mick Fleetwood (drums) and John McVie (bass).

This was by no means Fleetwood Mac's first visit to The Ritz, they had been playing there quite regularly as the blues band they then were (minus Kirwan) whilst promoting their Blue Horizon Record label albums *Fleetwood Mac* and *Mr. Wonderful* along with the accompanying singles.

But the band's then latest 45 *Albatross* had been released the month before and when they were about to play it at the end of their set, Peter Green smiled as he introduced it and said, "This is our latest single, which seems to be creeping up the charts…" Of course, it hit the No.1 position not long after and the band went mega, so it was the last time we would see them on the relatively small stage at The Ritz, as the band went on, not only to play the stadiums of the world, but also suffer three personal casualties within their ranks with Green, Spencer and Kirwan, one way or another and for various reasons, leaving the band but those are other stories.

As an interesting nugget for guitarists, many years before electronic tuners Green would tune his guitar to The Beatles' *Day Tripper* riff and although not an accomplished guitarist myself, the notes when played are easier to recognise as being in or out of tune using this method. Green would quickly run through the riff across the fret board from time to time throughout the gig, often during a song introduction, just to check his tunings.

Bournemouth Echo **adverts for Fleetwood Mac at the Ritz**
Note: Interesting interpretation of *Albatross*

Simon Dupree & The Big Sound.

From nearby Portsmouth, where the three brothers in the band: Derek (vocals), Phil (vocals, saxophone and trumpet) and Ray Schulman (guitar, violin, trumpet and vocals), along with a bassist, drummer and keyboard player, were a fairly regular attraction at The Ritz. They had a No.8 chart hit with their 'Psychedelic Rock' track called *Kites* but were unable to follow it up (although their *Without Reservations* LP did fairly well) and disbanded to form Gentle Giant, whom enjoyed much more popularity as one of the fast-becoming-trendy 'Progressive Rock Bands'.

Amongst their other credits, they released a single titled *Broken Hearted Pirates*, which had an unaccredited Dudley Moore playing piano and hired a then unknown pianist named Reginald Dwight (Elton John) for their 1967 Scottish tour.

The Ritz.

This was a very homely, smoky, sticky-floored typical blues / jazz club on Bournemouth's West Cliff and was situated about 100 yards along to the right of The Pier as you face it looking out to sea. It had a very small foyer / cloakroom with a bar to the left with one stage set within a bay window to the right and another straight ahead to accommodate both the main and support bands. On that evening in February, Fleetwood Mac played on the stage furthest away and, as ever, the 6 foot-plus-tall Mick Fleetwood and the 5 feet or less Jeremy Spencer would walk through the crowd together (that's how the bands went onstage at The Ritz, with just the cloakroom to change in, if needs must) much to the amusement of the whole audience; they were typically 'the long and short of it'!

As ever when Fleetwood Mac had played there, school friend, Eric Billett (with whom most of these gigs would be attended) and I would make our way to the front of the stage (as the band would be helping pack up their own gear, I think they would have had one roadie / driver at the most back then) to have a chat with Jeremy Spencer, whom we both admired. Eric took great delight in offering Jeremy a cigarette (he smoked the 'Piccadilly' brand at the time, which I don't think are on sale these days) and took even greater delight when he accepted, as we stood there yarning about blues whilst finding out what was happening to Jeremy Spencer and Fleetwood Mac as we smoked.

The Ritz Ballroom
1969

The Ritz would also host appearances by Audience in the June and Van Der Graff Generator in December, and somewhere in between, or perhaps the previous year or the one following it, The Savoy Brown Blues Band, Chicken Shack, The Alan Bown, Juicy Lucy, The Nice and John Mayall's Bluesbreakers would also play there. The venue started out as a jazz club, with Chris Barber and his band and suchlike, but again, with the popularity of Pop and Blues such as it had become, the venue had to change with the times to attract the younger generation of punters.

Chicken Shack.

Chicken Shack were also another band visiting The Ritz on a regular basis. Like Fleetwood Mac, they were on the Blue Horizon Record label, and would have been promoting their *Okay Ken?* and the *40 Blue Fingers Freshly Packed* albums. Christine Perfect would also play *I Would Rather Go Blind* from her solo album, which featured that knockout single. She was very much admired as one of, if not *the* very first female artistes in a very much male-dominated world of late 1960s English blues.

What with Christine being from London where fashion was a month or two ahead of the rest of the UK and this being the first era of the mini or micro skirt and boys being boys, we would crowd the stage after the final encore to catch a glimpse of Christine's (usually white) laundry as she slid around and stood up from her piano stool. But obviously, she knew it was a huge tease to our slightly post-adolescent fantasies, as she could have modestly slid her knees the opposite way when making ready to stand to take a bow and thus cheating us of that nano-second 'flash'. But thankfully, she chose to titillate and in doing so, it probably went a long way into shifting a few extra LPs but then nobody, least of all us, were going to complain. In 1968, *Melody Maker* presented her with an award for having one of the Top 10 Best Pairs of Legs in Britain!

The Savoy Brown Blues Band.

The Savoy Brown Blues Band were quite something, too. They were all great musicians, though guitarist Kim Simmonds and Chris Youlden with his gritty vocals seemed to take the majority of the spotlight. And, of course, we would buy their LPs (Savoy Brown had some captivating artwork, especially on their *Looking In* and *Hellbound Train* album sleeves) and another school friend, Terry Best, would take along the inner paper sleeve from the LP for the band members to autograph.

Kim Simmonds was one of the first guitarists to be on the road using a Gibson 'Flying V' guitar, which later became popular with Wishbone Ash and on occasion also with Jimi Hendrix. Flying Vs were and are great to play standing up but when sitting down they tend to slide off the thigh and, if you're not quick, hitting the floor and breaking and without the benefit of Pete Townshend's prowess and showmanship for your pains, also your expense!

Savoy Brown's *Train To Nowhere* single was a hit in 1969 and became one of the standards which most of the pub-rock blues cover bands would play. It's a moderate tempo song with some light and delicate playing, along with some heavier riffing and musical highs and lows adding to its impact.

Chris Youlden had an amazing blues vocal and went on to record a few solo albums and has been invited to sing on an odd track here and there as a guest on other artistes' records.

Guitarist 'Lonesome' Dave Peverett, bass player Tony Stevens and drummer Roger Earl moved to America to find fame as Foghat.

Guitarist, Kim Simmonds has returned to the gigging circuit in these latter years with a blues band going under his own name. He played The Brook in Southampton a couple of years ago, as I noticed a poster advertising it whilst Eric and I were there at a Girlschool gig. We also met up with Terry Best again there at a Leslie West's Mountain gig, and also at later Yardbirds and Mountain gigs at Mr. Kyps in Parkstone. Terry has an incredible knowledge of the blues, and it's always great to bump into him.

The Alan Bown.

The Alan Bown were also an immense favourite and regular visitors to The Ritz but, whilst never having as deep Blues roots as so many other of Ritz regulars, The Alan Bown's brass section: Alan Bown himself on trumpet and John Anthony (Helliwell who would later move on to greater fame and fortune with Supertramp) on saxophone, gave them a far more R & B / Soul feel. But with Jess

66

Roden on vocals, they could never stray that far away, and if they did, Jess' brilliant Blues vocals would quickly bring them back again with songs like The Young Rascal's *You Better Run* and a pre-Jimi Hendrix version of Bob Dylan's *All Along The Watchtower* in their set.

However, when the 'flower power / psychedelic' boom was at its height, The Alan Bown embraced it completely with some fantastic songs to illustrate this absolutely unique piece of history we were lucky enough to be part of, not only because of the age we were and enjoying it, but living through it to tell the tale. With track titles like *Toyland, Magic Handkerchief, Story Book* and *Technicolour Dream* which they performed live bang-on-the-nail as good as their studio-recorded counterparts and which, incidentally, still stand up as being 'great' today they, if no one else, stamped the era with absolute psychedelic / hippie-trippy based pop perfection.

MGM Records Promotional Advert for *Toyland*

At the time, The Alan Bown, (who also featured Tony Catchpole on guitar, Stan Haldane on bass, Jeff Bannister on organ and piano and Vic Sweeney on drums), recorded for the MGM Record label, and their *Outward Bown* LP originally had been difficult to get hold of and as a vinyl LP was deleted for many years. But in 1998, See For Miles Records reissued the album on CD, with bonus tracks, plus the single and B-side of *Toyland* and *Technicolour Dream* in their original mono format. What an album it still is but only if you are old enough to appreciate it and can remember that amazing era perhaps.

Not too sure what happened to the remainder of the band, or even Alan Bown himself? As mentioned earlier, John Anthony (Helliwell) moved on to work with Supertramp throughout their massive and highly popular career and vocalist Jess Roden went on to achieve some success with bands he either joined or formed (like The Jess Roden Band and Bronco), before relocating to New York to work as a graphic designer - what a great pity and the waste of a superb voice but that's Rock 'n' Roll!

Robert Palmer (1949-2003) took over on vocals for a time until he joined singer Elkie Brooks in Dada and then Vinegar Joe, then with the Power Station, before finding himself a very successful solo career until his untimely and all-too early death.

The Nice.

The Nice were another band regular to The Ritz, and their *Thoughts Of Emerlist Davjack* album would provide the nucleus of their set, usually performed on the 'bay window' stage, which included their massive crowd pleaser / crowd puller and frantically-paced track titled *Rondo*. Members of The Nice, whose names were mixed and mingled within their album title, were Keith Emerson on keyboards, Lee Jackson on bass and vocals, David O'List on guitar, and Brian 'Blinky' Davidson (1942-2008) on drums. *Rondo* was actually derived from Dave Brubeck's *Blue Rondo a la Turk* composition and Emerson, a virtuoso keyboard player and showman (who later moved on to Emerson Lake and Palmer), particularly

Poster for The Nice Concert
The Winter Gardens, Bournemouth on 6th February 1970
Courtesy of the Bourne Beat Bar, Bournemouth

during *Rondo* but not exclusively, would 'stab' his Hammond organ keyboard with two Hitler Youth daggers, (gifted him by their then roadie Lemmy Kilmister, who later went on to play The Ritz with his psychedelic / blues band, Sam Gopal, and later onward again to find fame with Hawkwind and Motorhead). So whilst the daggers held the keys down, Emerson would hump and bump and even kneel on top of the organ 'riding it' around his section of the stage, creating wild feedback and, being the perfect showman, it was quite some spectacle to watch and enjoy. At other gigs, Emerson also set fire to the Hammond and along with the semi-destructive element already in place at all their shows he was dubbed by fans as 'The Jimi Hendrix of the Keyboards'.

The other The Nice showstopper, of course, was their version of Leonard Bernstein's *West Side Story* song *America*, integrated with parts of Dvorak's New World Symphony. Regarded by the band as a protest song against the US Bill of Rights provision for the Bearing of Arms, it was therefore released as *America (Second Amendment)* and with the Vietnam War and the 'Hippie Peace and Love' themes prevalent in every day living at the time, the single was a Top 40 chart hit, although radio play was restricted.

But with the blood-stirring *Rondo* and *America*, along with LP tracks like *Flower King Of Flies*, *War And Peace* and the album title track, plus the very hippie-influenced *America* B-side titled *The Diamond Hard Blue Apples Of The Moon*, The Nice were quite an act to see. But fame and fortune would follow on from these 'cosy' appearances at The Ritz and a year or so later the band would achieve greater status and play the Winter Gardens with hard-earned headlining shows on major UK tours and for Emerson, later, the major stadiums of the world with ELP.

Juicy Lucy.

Rather like The Who's *I Can See For Miles*, Juicy Lucy's Top 20 Hit with their supercharged rendition of Bo Diddley's *Who Do You Love?* made them an immediate favourite. Featuring the powerful vocal of Ray Owens and the superb razor-sharp and adrenaline-pumping, lap-steel slide guitar playing of American Glenn 'Fernando' Campbell, this band were also a 'must' to go and see at The Ritz.

Originally called The Misunderstood, they reputedly renamed themselves with the more 'hip' band name of 'Juicy Lucy' after the Malayan prostitute so-named in Leslie Thomas' *The Virgin Soldiers* novel.

Their debut LP on Vertigo Records was also something of a wow! With its gatefold sleeve featuring the naked burlesque dancer Zelda Plum covered in fruit, thereby depicting 'Juicy Lucy', album sleeves like these were regarded as quite risqué at the time and Juicy Lucy would be there side-by-side with the 19 or 20 naked women adorning Jimi Hendrix' double LP set *Electric Ladyland* as another one of the LPs those staid and boring Governmental old farts would try to ban for being 'indecent'.

But the band went down a storm at The Ritz and it would be their only appearance there, albeit it very hot and sweaty one, and that LP sleeve and the adrenaline-pumping rendition of *Who Do You Love?* along with *Mississippi Woman* from the same LP, will live on far longer than any of us mere mortals.

We Discover the New World of Stereo.

Gradually, stereo records began creeping into our record collection and despite having the choice of either stereo or mono LPs when we bought them, inevitably most record fans would plump for the stereo version to have a copy ready and waiting for such times as they could afford a hi-fi. Eric was the first to save up to buy himself one and on one occasion when I visited him, he was full of smiles, excited, and waved me into his bedroom to place a pair of Boots' (the Chemist) fairly reasonably priced and affordable stereo headphones on my head. "Have a listen to this!" he ordered, as he put the record player needle on side 1 of the eponymous *Emerson, Lake and Palmer* album. That was the first time I'd heard stereo properly and through stereo headphones it was magnificent! With our ears (obviously) perfectly spaced, Greg Lake, who had produced the album, had mastered this new stereo effect whereby the music, in this case from Keith Emerson's Moog Synthesiser, could be made to sound as if it was going from the left ear to the right (or indeed vice-versa) over the top of your head. Bloody Hell! Now I was smiling stupidly, too! We dug out other stereo albums like Cream's *Disraeli Gears* to listen to the effects, if any, there might be. The stereo sound was amazing but nothing like the 'fireworks', as we called them, experienced with the 'ELP' album. Again, the younger listener / music student of today takes such wild phasing effects for granted, and, even as old as we are now, it's great to be able to say we lived in a time when this technology first emerged and was brand new to the world.

These effects were similar to the sound of a railway train, aircraft, vehicle, or emergency vehicle siren approaching, passing and receding into the distance, and variations upon it, and is known as 'The Doppler Effect' after Christian Doppler, who proposed the scientific hypothesis in 1842. Only with the development of double tracked 'stereo' records and the appropriate twin-channel Hi-Fi and speakers could it be brought into reality in the recording studio, and subsequently, the record buyer's entertainment systems.

It also enabled the 'onstage layout' of a band to be mimicked within the now wide-open stereo landscape, with a brand new and exciting audio-arena brought into the home.

Ever looking to create new soundscapes for their music, Pink Floyd and Mike Oldfield, of *Tubular Bells* fame, also dabbled into and released 'quadraphonic' albums on vinyl. These were fine and the radical system was used in the live concert arenas, having PA speakers also situated to the rear of the concert venue, behind the audience, and thus creating an early 'surround-sound' system. Yet despite this groundbreaking innovation, the punter appeared happy with the stereophonic effect, as 'quad' didn't take-off, perhaps due to the human being wishing to enjoy the effect on headphones but only possessing two ears and not the required four which are essential for 'quad'!

If there was but one record producer who made the utmost of these stereo soundscapes, it had to be Roy Thomas Baker with the majority of Queen's early albums; The Who, Guns 'n' Roses, The Rolling Stones, The Cars, Foreigner and Lone Star are amongst a massive, almost who's who listing of top bands who sought his expertise. Baker would literally cause the music to fly from speaker to speaker on occasion, whilst filling the stereo void between the speakers with a rich, full and loud soundscape which the rock fan regards as their essential requirement in listening.

John Mayall's Bluesbreakers.

Blues man, John Mayall had become famous not only on the strength of his own performances but also due to having Eric Clapton (post-Yardbirds), Peter Green (pre-Fleetwood Mac) and the young Mick Taylor (pre-Rolling Stones) as his guitar players (much like The Yardbirds for seeing Eric Clapton, Jeff Beck and Jimmy Page through their ranks).

Just after leaving school and about to venture into the working world, we had a family holiday in Littlehampton in Sussex, which was handy for Dad as it was close to Goodwood Racecourse (not that he was always in the bookies, but he just enjoyed a little flutter now and again), where we spent one of the days.

Littlehampton didn't have a great deal going for it as far as a 16 year old music / Blues fan was concerned, but it did have a (just the one) record shop. With the hippie / flower power thing as strong as it was, I'd had the choice and just about enough money (they cost 19 shillings and 11 pence then - 99 of today's pence!) to buy an LP. This record shop had most of the current hits and albums any record buyer would want but owing to this ever-changing era I was undecided between The Mother's Of Invention *Freak Out* LP and John Mayall's Bluesbreakers with Eric Clapton, the now infamous 'Dandy' comic sleeve photo being on the cover. Bearing in mind this was the year before we started going to The Ritz, The Yardbirds were already part of our vocabulary but the Redland's College visit had also swayed us towards The Troggs and The Who were a big favourite. But, luckily, good sense prevailed (as far as I'm concerned, anyway, though some may not agree) and my money went on the *Bluesbreakers* LP and hence, when John Mayall played The Ritz, he was also regarded as 'a must' to go and see.

By this time, Clapton had left the Bluesbreakers to play with Cream, as had Peter Green (to form Fleetwood Mac) and in their wake, Mick Taylor had joined. The Ritz cloakroom had three semi-comfortable chairs adjacent to it and, either through laziness or the fact I had never been privileged to find an empty one before, I decided to sit down. Beside me sat this wavy-haired young man who, as far as I knew, was just another punter. He seemed quiet and, I admit, even I was far less outgoing then than I have become in later years when I'd strike up a conversation with just about anyone so we didn't speak. Therefore it was quite something when John Mayall and his then band walked onto The Ritz' stage to realise I had been sitting next to Mick Taylor!

But upon saying that, I never have been one for bugging people who are famous, or even asking for an autograph and although Terry Best generally had his LP inner sleeve signed by any and every band that played The Ritz, the rest of us were not in the habit of doing so. In all fairness, Terry didn't 'bug' the artistes. In fact he was not the only one who asked politely for autographs and I dare say most of the bands and artistes would have felt a little upset if no one had asked them to sign something. After all, this was what being famous was, is, and always will be about.

So, along with everyone else we saw at The Ritz, John Mayall with Mick Taylor played a darned good gig, but hang on a minute, yes, there was just the *one* band that played there who most certainly didn't play the white man!

And they were…

Status Quo!

They had released *Pictures Of Matchstick Men* in January 1968 and must have played The Ritz a short time after as 'the crowd' was of perhaps 50 people and the single had yet to achieve its Top 10 position of No.7, making the band a 'one-hit-wonder' if not quite yet a household name. The single was being played on the radio quite frequently and the band might well have already been on *Top of the Pops* as the crowd had been calling for *Matchstick Men* especially when they finished the first half of their set.

This made it something like a pub gig which Status Quo, like so many of their contemporaries, had been playing up until this point or perhaps they preferred their gigs in two halves so that they didn't have to pay a support band out of their fee. Anyway, the crowd, were still calling for *Matchstick Men* 30 minutes later when Quo walked back onstage to play for their second set.

"We can't play that one tonight," Mike (as he was then known) Rossi said, "the battery in me wha-wha's dead and we haven't got another one!"

Admittedly times were different then and when shops closed at 5 or 6pm, they closed, and there was no late night shopping so fair play, if they sent a roadie out to get a new battery he wouldn't have found one but, as a result, their failure to play their soon-to-be 'greatest hit' almost caused a riot!

The mood of the crowd, small as it was, noticeably changed from one of polite and expectant applause to one of comparative disappointment and for the remainder of that final hour the band was continually heckled for their soon-to-be trademark 'hit' single.

The Ritz gig was probably something of a learning curve for

Status Quo. In the first instance, it would have appeased the crowd if they had played *Pictures Of Matchstick Men* without the wha-wha pedal effect, even though it featured prominently in the song, it would have been better than not playing it at all. Secondly, it must have taught the band never to run out of batteries! However, by the end of the evening, they had turned the audience around with their then psychedelic brand of Pop / Rock and managed to win them over though many left the venue still muttering their disappointment at not hearing Quo's then most popular song.

The Pretty Things.

Making a change from The Ritz as a venue, The Pretty Things played the Poole Technical College Main Hall in 1968, promoting their *S F Sorrow* concept album. Now, if ever The Beatles and The Rolling Stones were a parental nightmare of how they *did not* want their sons to turn out or the kind of young man their daughter should *not bring home,* then The Pretty Things magnified those feelings a hundred-fold. (Their name was taken from Bo Diddley's *Pretty Thing* song.) The Pretty Things were everything our parents dreaded and they typified 'those beatnik types' to perfection as far as parents were concerned and we had been warned a million times to 'beware of those beatnik types'! However, we thought they were great and they were our heroes.

So, everyone had lied about where they would be that evening, and had perhaps even torn the advert from the local newspaper as an extra measure of secrecy. Yet amongst our friends, if we *didn't* have a ticket for that Pretty Things gig, then we would be regarded as most definitely 'square, man'!

You see, Lemmy Kilmister from Motorhead has the definition of Rock 'n' Roll to perfection, in that 'Rock 'n' Roll is the music your parents hate' and he is right! Whether it's Bill Haley or Little Richard, or The Pussy Cat Dolls or Eminem, if our parents told us to turn it down or off or both because it's annoying them and didn't want us

76

to buy it in the first place, then that's Rock 'n' Roll!

But this Pretty Things gig was something else; the band were already renowned for not being particularly wholesome and the air inside Poole Tech's main hall wreaked of dope the minute you walked inside and if you weren't smoking it per se then you were enjoying the effects by what has become known in recent years as 'passive smoking'. Well, everyone at that gig was stoned, passively or otherwise. In 1968, there were no laws about using strobe lighting and The Pretty Things had theirs going during the majority of the songs and people were feeling strange and being sick. Perhaps it was a bit of 'dope sickness' where people who had never smoked a joint before were drinking and getting stoned and the mixture of the two not being so good but it was quite a night to remember.

Along with tracks from the *S F Sorrow* concept album, we were treated to some of those earlier Pretties classics like *Rosalyn, Don't Bring Me Down* and *Buzz The Jerk*. Local 'covers' support band The Push (putting another local village, Morden, onto the Rock 'n' Roll map) added their slice of lunacy with a song which was fast becoming their trademark around the local circuit. They used to play a cover of the Chris Montez hit *Let's Dance,* but changed the lyrics to 'baby, baby, won't you take a chance, and put your hands down my underpants and Let's Dance…' which, as corny as it was, it went down well with their followers at the time.

Greg Lake, Robert Fripp & King Crimson.

The year of 1969 would also bear witness once more to the fact that you didn't have live in or be from the London area to become a top-line recording and performing band, when King Crimson, with Robert Fripp and Greg Lake, who had both grown up and lived in the neighbouring towns of Wimborne and Oakdale (a suburb of Poole) hit the big time with their first album for Island Records with the incredible *In The Court Of The Crimson King* (it achieved No.2 in the UK chart). The album, with its characteristic once remembered never forgotten, wide open mouthed screaming face painted in vivid pink LP sleeve artwork would bring song titles like *The Court Of The Crimson King* and 21st *Century Schizoid Man* into both our consciousness and vocabulary, and also the moody and magnificent sound of a new piece of musical kit called the mellotron. King Crimson were the band of the moment and with two of its musicians from our local area this was something to be very proud of. The band made their second live appearance as guests to The Rolling Stones at their free Hyde Park concert in July 1969, in front of over a quarter of a million people and received a standing ovation after completing their set. They did not have a recording contract at the time but after the performance they had record companies making them all sorts of extraordinary offers, but finally settled for a contract with Island Records.

Local hearsay declared and gave much credence to a local guitar tutor, a Mrs. Gartside from a neighbouring village of Corfe Mullen, as being one of the best local tutors, when it came to be known that Robert Fripp had studied with her. Now, if any proof was required of her talent, this shows she obviously had it in volumes. Needless to say, her already full books were overflowing within a matter of hours from the news breaking in the local evening paper, and the small town of Wimborne had also now stamped its existence on the music scene of the younger generation. Also, local people had started talking not only about King Crimson but also Robert Fripp and Greg Lake. Some of our friends had gone to school with them, my father worked at the local Hamworthy Engineering factory and knew Harry Lake, Greg's father who would (at a later date, more so during the Emerson, Lake and Palmer era) bring in gold discs for his work colleagues to marvel at.

Although Mrs. Gartside was the stuff of local legend, and this rumour indeed was prevalent, she may well have tutored Fripp at one time, but other more accurate tales now tell of Fripp and Lake meeting up when they were both being tutored by Don Strike, in the small room behind his guitar shop in Westbourne Arcade. In essence it means little unless anyone remembers the late Don Strike personally as I do. When I visited his shop during my guitar-making era to buy that bass guitar fret board (pick-ups and machine heads at later dates) I marvelled at how the frets were so perfectly level. You see, I had also made an acoustic six-string at school during our woodwork classes and much to the disappointment of our woodwork teacher Mr. Buck, a bearded, mop-haired and be-spectacled folk music fanatic who begrudged my guitar making (a true exponent of this art would be known as a Luthier) as it rolled over into a second year and thus holding back the progress of my GCSE work.

But there was and is a lot involved in making a guitar, and we only had two lessons a week (perhaps a whole morning?) and the body front, back and sides had to not only be fashioned and assembled but also veneered and I wanted to and did give it my very best shot. Mr. Buck had chastised me on more than one occasion as my wood turning on the lathe had subsequently suffered at the expense of the guitar. But I didn't care! The guitar was far more essential than a few wood-turned fruit bowls and table lamps as far as I was concerned. And along with the lengthy process of applying veneer, I also had to buy the fret wire from Poole Music Stores in town whose staff cut enough to fret a six-string acoustic guitar from a *roll!* So, of course, every inch of the fret wire was *curved* from being housed on this roll and then it had to be cut, slightly over-length and then tapped into the appropriate slot in the fret board with a small hammer, gradually smoothed down with a file and then checked for level in relation to the others with a steel rule. Therefore, this is the reason why I marvelled at such accuracy from this experience in the classroom, when Mr. Strike handed me a perfectly made fret board ready to glue on to the guitar neck I had built at home.

"Ha-Ha!" smiled Mr. Strike, "putting frets into a fret board is a bit like changing the tyre on a motorbike, as soon as you've done it a few dozen times, you've learned quite a few tricks!" And he wasn't wrong, even though I didn't ever need to fret another guitar.

Unit Four & Oakdale Youth Club.

Greg Lake had started at the same place as every musician, at the bottom and Robert Fripp remembered the first time he heard Greg and his band named Unit Four auditioning for The Cellar Club in Market Street, Poole in 1965. (Later it was known as The Georgian Club and now after various other name changes, is currently known as The Blue Boar.) Afterwards we bumped into the band a few more times when they played gigs at Greg's local Oakdale Youth Club. (As mentioned earlier, The Cellar Club also hosted a gig by, amongst many others, Steampacket and once had a photo of the band on the wall in The Cellar. Steampacket were Long John Baldry [1941-2005], Rod Stewart, Vic Briggs, Julie Driscoll and Brain Auger. As The Blue Boar, this venue still hosts gigs by local bands today in the very same cellar, a completely brick lined hall with a high, curved ceiling, which is situated beneath the pub / restaurant).

The Blue Boar in Market Street, Poole
Formerly The Cellar Club

The Time Checks.

When Unit Four split up, as fledgling bands are apt to do, Greg formed The Time Checks, bringing in drummer Tony Bates and also Don Strike's son Bev on guitar (who carried on the family business after his parents passed away and still runs the guitar shop today with his wife, Lisa).

Greg Lake went on to play with The Gods, who later became Uriah Heap. However, he made no records with them, but singles were released by his next two bands.

The Cheerful Insanity of Giles, Giles and Fripp.

Whilst Greg Lake was with The Gods, Robert Fripp released an oddly obscure album, in 1968, which pointed towards his Jazz-tinged future titled *The Cheerful Insanity of Giles, Giles and Fripp*. The music on the album was very avant-garde and off-the-wall and similar to the free-form, freak-out, experimental Rock being played at around the same time on the other side of the Atlantic by Frank Zappa, The Mother's of Invention and Captain Beefheart. The album was largely ignored at the time of release, as the UK record buyer would only pick up on this genre of music a couple years later, when Radio 1 DJ John Peel (1939-2004) played tracks from what some regarded as this 'freaky music' on his late evening show.

Despite the pessimism of the general rock fan and even Decca Records who released the LP *The Cheerful Insanity* album sold 500 copies in its day, but is, nevertheless, still currently available on compact disc.

However, despite this comparative lack of interest, they would record another LP under the guise of Giles, Giles and Fripp titled *The Brondesbury Tapes* (which would not be released until 2001) when Peter Giles was replaced by Greg Lake on bass, after which the band then moved on to re-name themselves King Crimson, to receive world wide-critical acclaim and massive record sales.

The Shame.

The Shame comprised Greg Lake's Unit Four keyboard player John Dickenson, drummer Billy Nims and bassist Malcolm Brasher. As The Shame, they had an MGM Records single released in 1967, titled *Don't Go Away Little Girl / Dreams Don't Bother Me*, which featured Greg on guitars and lead vocals.

Shy Limbs.

Shy Limbs CBS single, recorded in 1968 and released in 1969, had *Reputation* as the A-side and *Love* as its flip and featured Greg Lake on guitars and lead vocals, John Dickenson keyboards and vocals, Malcolm Brasher bass and vocals and Andy McCullough on drums.

Both The Shame and Shy Limbs were keyboard-driven bands, similar to the Traffic and Procol Harum sound in later years, with excellent vocals, melody, lead guitar and plenty of psychedelic phasing and panning making full use of the then new stereo technology.

(Should anyone be interested in these early 45s, they were re-released on CD in 1997 as *From The Underground - The Official Bootleg* by Greg Lake on the Greg Lake Ltd Recordings Record label, with tracks from The Shame, Shy Limbs, King Crimson, Emerson, Lake & Palmer, Asia, Emerson, Lake & Powell and The Greg Lake Band.)

Greg had progressed onward and into the ranks of King Crimson with his pal, Robert Fripp, from those early bands and Bournemouth and its surrounding villages, rural and 'in the sticks' as they may well have been, were now on the Rock 'n' Roll map forever.

King Crimson played The Winter Gardens several times to packed houses of proud and enthralled local rock fans as well as friends and family of Greg and Robert. But Greg Lake would only stay with them for two albums *In The Court Of The Crimson King* and for vocals only on *In The Wake Of Poseidon*, before moving on to join that keyboard wizard from The Nice, Keith Emerson and Atomic

Poster for Emerson, Lake and Palmer Concert
The Winter Gardens, Bournemouth on 6th April 1971
Courtesy of the Bourne Beat Bar, Bournemouth

Rooster and Crazy World of Arthur Brown drummer, Carl Palmer as the super-group, Emerson, Lake and Palmer or ELP.

Emerson, Lake & Palmer.

They would record a string of very successful albums: *Emerson, Lake and Palmer* in 1971, and *Tarkus* in 1972 and Greg Lake's song writing mastery would be highlighted with *Just Take A Pebble* and *Lucky Man* (which he had written at school) from those albums.

All through Greg's career he has taken with him the keyboard influence which was prevalent even on those early singles, moving into the Mellotron sound during the King Crimson years and, of course, with Keith Emerson in ELP and Geoff Downes in Asia.

But in 1975, Lake released one of if not *the* best Christmas singles of all time, ensuring his name would live well beyond the grave with *I Believe In Father Christmas*. With stunning lyrics from King Crimson maestro Pete Sinfield on this track, Greg played bass, guitars and sung the lead vocal, whilst being spectacularly joined by Godfrey Salmon as the conductor of The London Philharmonic Orchestra and The King's Singers. Not originally intended for release as a single and despite Sinfield's lyrics (from which some have regarded it as 'The atheist's Christmas song') it has been released every year since and featured on a myriad of festive-themed albums and made Greg Lake a household name; the lad from Oakdale has done good!

Much like Pete Brown, Martin Sharp and Mike Taylor (1938-1969) who had written lyrics for Eric Clapton, Jack Bruce and Ginger Baker during Cream's first and most famous era, Peter Sinfield conjures quirky, cinematic images within his lyrics for King Crimson, Emerson Lake and Palmer and Greg Lake. All 4 writers excel at this style of Rock lyric writing, where they paint immense pictures with very few words, and then change that picture to another of equal or surpassed imagery with another few sparse words. This is quite an astounding art form and within which only these lyricists are masters.

Transit Sound.

The October 21st 1968 edition of the *Bournemouth Evening Echo* ran a small feature on Wimborne based group Transit Sound saying that they had done well in a local competition considering their age. Detailed as Steve Evans, aged 15, on lead guitar, Gary Margetts also 15 on rhythm guitar and vocals, Tristian Margetts, aged 13, on bass guitar and Tony Brock on drums; they were pupils from Henry Harbin School. They would evolve into…

Spontaneous Combustion.

When Emerson, Lake and Palmer played Bournemouth's Winter Gardens on November 10th 1972 with their *Tarkus* LP UK Tour, they took Wimborne based rockers Spontaneous Combustion with them as support band. Their *Spontaneous Combustion* (Harvest Records SHVL 801) and *Triad* (Harvest SHVL 805) albums had both been produced by Greg Lake and released in 1971 and 1972 respectively.

Spontaneous Combustion track listing: *Speed Of Light / Listen To The Wind / Leaving / 200 Lives / Down With The Moon / Reminder.*

Triad track listing: *Spaceship / Brainstorm / Child Life / Love & Laughter / Pan / Rainy Day / Monolith Parts 1, 2 & 3.* (Both albums were also re-released on one CD in 1997, by See For Miles Records).

From their humble beginnings playing at Wimborne Youth Club, to being the guests of ELP on a full scale UK tour was a dream come true for Spontaneous Combustion, a three-piece band made up of Gary Margetts, guitar and vocals, brother Tristian (Tris) Margetts, bass and vocals and Tony Brock on drums. Along with the above LPs, they had also released 3 singles for the Progressive Rock Harvest Record label: *Lonely Singer / 200 Lives / Leaving* (HAR 5046) 1971, *Gay Time Night / Spaceship* (HAR 5060) 1972 and *Sabre Dance Parts 1 & 2* (HAR 5066) in 1973.

The gig was pretty good and back then punters actually took the time to sit and watch the 'up-and-coming' support bands because you never knew if there might be a nice surprise on the way. These days punters generally just stay in the bar, believing *every* support band to be crap. But everyone deserves a chance and the pecking order dictates a band begins as a support act and works their way up, if indeed they have the talent to do so.

Time.

Yet despite Greg Lake's connection, Spontaneous Combustion did not hit the big time during a period in Rock history when such a vast number of so-called 'Progressive Rock outfits' were recording, treading the boards and pulling out all the stops to become famous. So, with Tris, on bass and vocals again and Gary, once more on guitar and vocals, they moved on to record an album under the name of *Time*, with Mike Udell on lead vocals, Alex Johnson on guitar and vocals, and Jodie Leigh on drums, vibes, timpani and vocals for the BUK Records label (BULP 2005) – 1975 LP which was produced by Conny Plank at The House Of Sounds for BUK Records Ltd. The album goes for 'silly money' in collector's circles and on EBay.

Time - vinyl LP - all songs written by GW Margetts & HE Yeatman.

Side 1: *Shady Lady* / *Turn Around* / *Violence* / *Yesterday, Today, Tomorrow*.

Side 2: *Dragonfly* / *Liar* / *Hideout* / *Steal Away*.

The Greg Lake Band.

With their friendship still sailing high, Greg Lake would later have Tris Margetts in his Greg Lake Band (with guitarist Gary Moore playing Bournemouth's Winter Gardens on October 25th 1981) but Gary Margetts apparently quit the music business altogether whilst drummer Tony Brock would go on to play with Strider, The Babys and in the 1980s as the drummer for Rod Stewart's backing band.

Emerson, Lake and Palmer would go on, album by album, to

become megastars around the world achieving some 30 million units of record sales. Their 1974 *triple* LP *Welcome Back My Friends, To The Show That Never Ends* achieved No.4 in the American charts, and was one of only a few *triple LP sets* to have ever done so.

Tracks Greg Lake had also written were massively popular and *From The Beginning* was released from its trilogy parent album as a single to achieve No.39 in the American Billboard chart. *Lucky Man* and *Take A Pebble* were and are still great favourites along with that blood-stirring epic *Fanfare For The Common Man* from the 1977 *Works Volume 1* album.

As another note of interest, Greg Lake replaced John Wetton for a period of time in the band, Asia, and although Wetton was born in Derbyshire, he had been brought up in Poole and had been friends with Robert Fripp during their school days. John also worked with King Crimson from 1972 to 1974 appearing on the albums *Larks Tongues In Aspic* and *Starless And Bible Black*. But with both Lake and Wetton being great vocalists and bass guitarists, it was easy to move into each others' positions within these bands.

Al Stewart.

1969 would also be the year folk guitarist / singer Al Stewart released his second album *Love Chronicles*. Amongst other talented artistes Al had recruited to record this album, Yardbirds guitarist Jimmy Page had played some guitar on it. And huge Yardbirds fans as we were, we had been to the pictures (The Regent Cinema, in Poole) and watched the rare Yardbirds line-up with both Jimmy page and Jeff Back when it had been featured in the film, starring David Hemmings, Vanessa Redgrave and Sarah Miles, titled *Blow Up*.

The year before, when Eric had passed his driving test, he had taken me to one such used record shop in Westbourne, which at the time was named Jon's Exchange & Mart. The shop was a cornucopia of good condition but used goods, like 8mm movie cameras and projectors, amplifiers and guitars; you name it. Long before the credit card was even thought of, Exchange & Mart shops like this thrived in buying, when people were hard-up or had a bill to pay and needed 'instant cash', and selling it back when they were flush. Much as the guitars and amps would prove to be interesting in later years, Eric and I would visit to look through the second hand LPs.

Of course, we got to know the owner Jon Kremer whose father Monty also had a similar shop in nearby Moordown, which we would visit from time to time for the same reason. But inside Jon's shop one Saturday afternoon I pulled out the *Love Chronicles* album. Jon's eyes sparkled and a huge smile beamed across his face as he took the LP to then draw my attention to the inside of the album's gatefold sleeve. Thinking he would be showing me the Jimmy Page connection, Jon pointed to his own name Jonny Kremer, within the 'thanks' section. He then told me the delightful story of how it came to be there.

"I met up with Al in my father's (Monty's) shop," Jon enlightened me. "He'd been on the bus from Wimborne to Bournemouth and noticed a guitar reverb unit in the shop window. From that meeting we became friends and learned to play guitar together. Al was a fairly accomplished player already and my Dad had started teaching me some Shadow's tunes. We remained friends and later on Al played a one-off gig in Tony Blackburn's backing group, The Sabres, (on June 21st 1963 at the Pavilion), who in turn, were support band for another well-respected Bournemouth musician, Zoot Money. (Tony Blackburn lived in Poole and studied at Bournemouth Tech. He later became a pirate radio and then a Radio 1 DJ.)

Jon and Al Stewart also knew and learned guitar with another Bournemouth-based musician, Andy Summers, who was guitarist in two of the local bandleader, Zoot Money's groups, those being his Big Roll Band and also the 'psychedelically influenced' Dantalion's Chariot. (Andy Summers, of course, would later team up with Gordon Sumner [Sting] and Stewart Copeland to form and achieve worldwide fame and acclaim as The Police).

This was interesting stuff, even for 1969, as it was great to hear about other musicians from the area making a name for themselves in the 'difficult' world of music. But Al had become bored with Beat Groups, had fallen under the influence of Bob Dylan and had already left Bournemouth to seek fame and recognition on the UK folk club circuit. He became significantly adept at his craft to gain a contract with CBS Records, which was no mean feat for a 'solo' performer.

The *Love Chronicles* album was regarded as one of the 'must-have' records in the collection of the aspiring rebel. It was and still is a damned fine record as a whole and the Jimmy Page 'session musician' appearance was also regarded as being quite something. But it also had the 'F' word within the lyrics of the 18 minute title track and for 1969 that was risqué and made it all the more appealing. So it was a great move to own a copy and it also give a silent 'up yours' to the parents in the hope that they might hear the word and get annoyed about it, thus increasing ones 'rebel' stance and attitude even more.

After several more successful albums, Al's subsequent move to Los Angeles some years later brought with it the immense success of his *Year Of The Cat* album and despite the fact that he was born in Scotland, but had moved with his family to the Bournemouth area, his glory of being yet another 'local boy done good' was escalated all the more when that album shot him into 'superstar' status by selling in bucket loads.

Al and Jon, of course, have remained friends to this day, with Al returning to the UK to gig from time to time and Eric playing the chauffeur by driving Jon, often accompanied by his artist wife Abi, to meet up again, catch up on old times and enjoy one or more of his gigs fairly local to the area.

Zoot Money.

George Bruno 'Zoot' Money is a singer, pianist, organist, band leader and actor who was born in Bournemouth in 1942. Inspired by Jerry Lee Lewis and Ray Charles, he soon became part of the vibrant local scene and in 1961 formed his 'Big Roll Band' with Andy Summers on guitar. They were a popular live attraction on the London scene with the Blues and R & B 'in crowd' well into the 'Swinging Sixties'. Then becoming known as Blues Incorporated and in 1967 as Dantalian's Chariot, Zoot is a well respected musician and has always flown the flag for Bournemouth.

Zoot Money at The Flamingo Club, Wardour Street, London, 1964
Andy Summers is second from the right.

Blow Up and All My Loving.

Blow Up was a controversial 'Swinging 60s London' movie made by Michelangelo Antonioni in 1966 and a showcase for The Yardbirds, although the remainder of the soundtrack music, played by Herbie Hancock, would remain Jazz-orientated. The movie, with David Hemmings as photographer Thomas, was winner of the 1966 Best Picture and Director Awards. The enlargements (*Blow Up's*) Thomas made of photographs he discretely took of what he thought were an innocent romantic couple in a park actually reveal the female (played by Vanessa Redgrave) apparently positioning the male to be murdered by a shadow-like figure with a gun in the surrounding bushes and he becomes obsessed with finding out the truth.

Thomas is also featured with a young and blonde model, Jane Birkin (who had a No.1 single, regarded by the elder generations as 'sexually explicit' in 1969, *Je 'taime…moi non plus* with Serge Gainsbourg) and a brunette model friend Gillian Hills in a three-way giggly schoolgirl-like bi-sexual romp. He moves on to a pretty far-out drugs orgy and then stumbles across The Yardbirds playing at the Marquee Club, with Jeff Beck smashing up his guitar. Rather than continue with the plot and spoil it if you've not watched it, the DVD is recommended.

The film was based on a short story about real-life photographer, David Bailey and was controversial at the time for its sexual content as it was the first British film to feature full frontal female nudity.

For Yardbirds fans, this was a particularly historic performance as it captured the band with both Jeff Beck and Jimmy Page in the line-up. Antonioni actually wanted The Who for the movie, but they were committed elsewhere at the time. This knowledge explains Beck's uncharacteristic guitar smashing routine, which was essential to the plot of the story.

Going to see *Blow Up* at The Regent Cinema in Poole High Street mainly for The Yardbirds inclusion, the film seemed to set up a lifelong fascination for films where I was left wondering 'what was that all about?' as the end credits rolled. Rather like *The Usual Suspects*, *Vanishing Point* and *Jacob's Ladder* in later years, *Blow Up* for me required several viewings to get to the root of what I considered to be quite a deep, mysterious and complex plot. Perhaps it's just that I'm thick, but this aspect at least gives a film longevity and I watch these four films fairly regularly even today. *Blow Up* is a classic timepiece reflecting 1960s London exactly as it was during that era, and for that reason alone is essential viewing for younger generations to enjoy a taste of that period in British history.

Tony Palmer, who filmed Cream's 1968 Albert Hall Farewell Gig, also made a TV documentary filmed in 1968 and screened in 1969 titled *All My Loving*, which has recently been released on DVD. Featuring Cream, The Who, Jimi Hendrix, Pink Floyd, The Beatles, Eric Burdon and many more stars of the day both in concert and interview. Much like *Blow Up*, it is a vivid snapshot of then 'Pop' scene as it was changing shape and subdividing into Rock music and its associated facets. Also included is newsreel footage from the era, mainly of the Vietnam War and the Paris student riots, as well as other then current events, making this an excellent social documentary for a student or journeyman of the era.

Derek & The Dominoes.

Bournemouth would not only be astounded, but also honoured when Eric Clapton's then latest band, Derek and the Dominoes, played The Pavilion Ballroom on August 18th, 1970. Cream had played the venue at very short notice in August 1966* and I'd only heard about it afterwards (from Eric's friend, Richard Tong, who commented about Ginger Baker tapping the bar top with a pint beer glass, asking the barmaid for a refill, please!), so Clapton playing the town again (although the band would return to play The Winter Gardens on October 7th), this show was an absolute 'must' to go and see.

The *Layla And Other Assorted Love Songs* album wasn't released until the December of that same year, and the *Layla* track as a single had to wait until 1972, so we must have been very fortunate to have had the *Layla* song played on that hot summer evening. It can easily be remembered as being played, as virtually no other song around that time had such an extended piano solo. But this band thrilled the audience, known at this time as 'The Pavi People', as the venue liked to refer to us in their advertising.

Both Eric and another school pal, Alan Plummer, from Sturminster Marshall, attended this gig. It was a joy to see and hear a lifelong hero such as Eric Clapton in our hometown of Bournemouth, especially after missing the very low-key Cream gig.

[*There is no advertised 'proof' of Cream's Pavilion gig by way of an *Evening Echo* advertisement (although Eric remembers it as 'about the size of a postage stamp'), a ticket stub, or indeed any verification within the published itineraries found in their biographies. All we have is the hearsay of local people who attended the gig, or remember it taking place. Eric remembers it happened on a Monday not long after Cream's official live debut at the 6th National Jazz & Blues Festival appearance at Royal Windsor racecourse in Berkshire on July 31st 1966 where his friend, Richard Tong, had watched them. Richard then went to see Cream again at The Pavilion gig, only telling Eric about it after the event and likewise, him telling us. Another local friend of Eric's, John Sharman, was the Pavilion DJ at the time and also recalls the show being on a Monday night. This seems to point to the gig being played at the Pavilion Ballroom on Monday August 8th 1966.

From Chris Welch's Cream biography:

"At Windsor, Cream caused a sensation playing *Spoonful*, *Traintime* and *Stepping Out*. It was clear that here was the biggest new band of the year. So it seemed odd that they were now saddled with a string of small club dates that had been booked in advance for little (£45 a night) money."

Bournemouth Pavilion was one of those gigs Cream were

'saddled with' but without that 'proof' their Tour Diary will remain incomplete.

Richard Tong remembers, "It was probably the greatest gig I ever attended, I was within feet of Clapton for most of the performance."

Nick Churchill at the *Bournemouth Daily Echo* has written several features in the paper trying to track down the date of this mystery gig. Many local rock fans remember it, but without that printed proof of the date we are confounded.]

Bright Lights, Big City - Cream's Farewell Show at The Royal Albert Hall.

However, in 1968, when at Poole Technical College studying 'O' levels, a hairy and bearded young man named Nigel, who was the Student Union boss, pinned flyers on the notice boards throughout the college with words roughly to this effect: Cream's Farewell Gig, The Royal Albert Hall, in London, on November 26th, if you would like to go, send for a ticket, (the Royal Albert Hall Box Office address was given), present it to Nigel as proof we were going, and he would then arrange to hire a minibus to take us there.

The ticket prices varied from 12/6d (38p today), to the most expensive, I believe, was 30/- (£1.50).

After my tip-off about this, school friend, Terry Best, whom I had also worked with at Poole Park's nursery where we were junior gardeners, also bought a ticket for himself and then girlfriend, Jeanne. Along with Nigel and 8 others, we crammed into a 12 seat minibus; the Cream Fans from Poole were dropped off outside The Royal Albert Hall on the appropriate evening.

As was the custom at the time, the Cream Farewell show actually played two houses, an early and a late, and even though we had quite some distance to travel and despite the fact the early performance would have suited us better, it had sold out by the time we bought our tickets. So we either had to enjoy the privilege of attending Cream's very last and final second performance and arrive home late or not go at all. Having missed their Bournemouth Pavilion gig, here they were 27 months later playing their final gig. My soul would not have rested easy in my grave had I not taken this final opportunity to see them and I think that went for everyone who attended those last 2 shows. Cream had been *the band to see* as soon as their creation had been announced, a trio of exceptional talent: Eric Clapton, Jack Bruce and Ginger Baker. *They were* the first Super-Group and *they were* the band of our generation whom everyone wanted to see at least once. That final chance could not have been passed by; we would have crawled on our hands and knees had it been the only way of getting there.

The support bands were both on their way up the ladder of fame and in division 3 (earning a living by playing the circuit, with a record contract) and about to hit the big(ger) time with this guest slot supporting the sadly about to become defunct Cream. Those support bands were Yes and Taste and both were very impressive to say the least. Yes, of course, had their technically brilliant guitarist in Steve Howe and Taste, from Ireland, had the relatively unknown but nevertheless excellent Rory Gallagher (1948-1995) as their guitarist. I'm pretty sure they both had first LPs out at this time, Taste had *On The Boards* most definitely and played tracks from it, but added in a 'never recorded or released' stunning instrumental of George Gershwin's *Summertime* which was something of a showstopper.

A modern-day replica poster of Cream's Farewell Gig (selling at £15 and a rip-off) incorrectly has Taste billed as 'Rory Gallagher' due to his subsequent 'solo' name being far more famous than 'Taste'.

Yes had their first, self-titled LP out, but Steve Howe played his legendary guitar work-out, titled *The Clap* (into which he integrated most of Mason Williams' 1968 hit single, *Classical Gas*), which would appear 2 LPs further on in their career, on *The Yes* album in 1971. Up-and-coming DJ John Peel was master of ceremonies.

Of course, despite the band saying otherwise, Cream were superb as far as those whom attended were concerned, and their performance was recorded and broadcast on BBC 1 TV on January

5th, 1969 as *The Cream Farewell Concert*. This would subsequently be released on VHS tape and later on DVD, exactly as it had been shown on the television at the time. And great as we thought it was, it had been treated as a documentary, so short sections of the songs were 'ruined' with Patrick Allan's (1927-2006) narration. Another, slightly better DVD was later released with the original broadcast, plus several more full length versions of some of the songs. During the course of reviewing these releases on the Amazon website, I asked if the *original film* the BBC shot at the concert, from the moment the band walked on stage through to when they walked off, *without* Patrick Allen's now corny and out-of-date dialogue, could be released in its entirety so that those of us who attended (now aged mid-50s or older) *are still alive and are able to watch and enjoy it.* Thus far, my challenge has not been taken up and I doubt it ever will but it would be something of a superb release for everyone concerned, whether they had attended the show or not.

But that was an 'Out Of Town' gig and the first I had attended in London. We enjoyed it immensely and it would go down as one of our 'gigs of a lifetime'. If you know where to look, as we do, there are photos in Cream's biographies by Chris Welch and Dave Thompson in which Terry, Jeanne and I can be seen quite clearly (we were sitting to the right behind Eric Clapton with our backs against the first barrier). The idea of buying a copy of the photo to frame has often crossed my mind. It is available from the Pictorial Press photo agency but at £75 it will have to wait for a 60th Birthday present or other similar grand event.

We were picked up outside the venue by our mini bus driver and driven home to arrive back in the small hours to be questioned rigorously by mum and dad, who probably thought by going to a show in London we had been plied with and been forced to take LSD and suchlike and were now raving junkies. This, however, was not the case but we were stricken with a mixture of emotions, on the one hand being extremely fired up with adrenaline after attending Cream's *actual, final, last ever show* and on the other, feeling gutted that Clapton, Baker and Bruce would never perform live again as our beloved Cream!

With the then unknown media of VHS video, or indeed DVD even an imagined pipe-dream at the time, I desperately needed to capture some sort of souvenir of Cream's final show as a keepsake of my attendance. It was the first concert I had ever attended that had been filmed, never mind subsequently televised.

So, when it was shown on TV, with brother Robert away at University, I packed mum and dad off to bed early as I wanted to record it as best I could. Using the trusty reel-to-reel tape recorder, with a 12" ruler beneath the heavy family dictionary on top of the TV set, I dangled the microphone from the overhanging ruler right in front of the TV speaker. This, surely, would give me the best possible recording? And it did, well a pretty fair one anyway and much better than nothing. And that was it until probably in the late 1980s, when they released it on VHS tape.

The set played at the 2nd Royal Albert Hall show was: *White Room / Politician / I'm So Glad / Sitting On Top Of The World / Crossroads / Toad / Spoonful / Sunshine of Your Love / Stepping Out.*

(Cream reformed in May 2005 to play 4 shows, again at The Royal Albert Hall, which I did not attend as I believed it would perhaps spoil my memories of the original, final show. But I have thoroughly enjoyed this reunion show since on the DVD release. And although watching one of my all-time favourite-band's reunion on DVD was a great experience, I still felt my decision in not attending was the right thing to do. It also gave someone, who perhaps didn't make it to the 1968 show, or were not even born then, *my seat,* in which they no doubt thoroughly enjoyed the performance).

Eric Clapton when with Cream, 1967
playing his psychedelically painted Gibson SG guitar

Poster for Derek and The Dominoes Concert
The Pavilion, Bournemouth on 18th August 1970
Courtesy of the Bourne Beat Bar, Bournemouth

Beat Instrumental / Eric Clapton's Cream SG Guitar.

This glossy monthly magazine was the best we had on the news stands in the 1960s. The *NME, Melody Maker, Record Mirror* and *Disc & Music Echo* were great publications on a weekly basis but *Beat Instrumental* was *the essential* and just about the only monthly purchase for the rock fan. Often, it was worth buying simply for the coloured photo on the front cover and this would be the case when an issue featured Cream's Eric Clapton playing his psychedelically painted Gibson SG guitar in 1967. This was *the* guitar of the hippie era and still is *the* guitar of the hippie generation.

While at Poole College at this time studying for 'O' Levels, a fellow student named Sue Huxter who sported boyishly short bleached-blonde hair and was suitably micro-mini-skirted 'of the era' strutted into our common room waving the Clapton edition of *Beat Instrumental* in everyone's face, promising to paint the picture of Clapton with this amazing guitar in oils as soon as she possibly could. Just looking at the artwork on that guitar was and still is absolutely breathtaking and is unique in capturing the absolute spirit of the weird yet beautiful English hippie era in one solitary statement.

The painting on the front body of the guitar has been described as: "A winged wood sprite with curls of fire sat astride a cotton candy cloud. The left hand holds a triangle, whilst the right holds a spoon-shaped beater about to strike it. The arch of his right foot is balanced atop the tone control, while the toes of his left points delicately downwards towards the pick-up toggle switch. Yellow six-pointed stars are sprinkled against a sky of azure orbiting him, whilst swirls, flames and gradient shades of blues, greens and yellows dance across the instrument's body. An orange orb, dipped behind a burnt sienna mountain range floats across the pick-guard."

The guitar, known today as 'The Fool' after the Dutch artists and musicians, Simon Posthuma and Marijke Koger, whom had psychedelically designed and painted not only the exterior of The

Beatles London Apple offices, but also clothing and LP sleeves for Procol Harum, The Hollies, The Incredible String band and The Move had also recorded an eponymous album which was produced by Hollies' Graham Nash. Overawed and impressed with every brush stroke the couple had made and with Clapton being *the* hippie fashion icon, he fell under the influence of Simon and Marijke's art and asked them to use their trippy, acid-influenced painting skills on Cream's instruments. There are photos of Jack Bruce's bass and Ginger Baker's drums in practically all of the Cream biographies, but it would be Eric's SG which would achieve iconic status.

Clapton had used a 3-pick-up Gibson Les Paul guitar during his tenure with John Mayall's Bluesbreakers and would also use it to record the *Fresh Cream* album. But then it was stolen, so Clapton decided upon, tried out and bought a cherry painted Gibson SG, and it would be this guitar that 'The Fool' painted and would be shown off to the British hippies of the day for the first time in colour on the *Beat Instrumental* cover. It made its actual public debut on the *Murray the K* American TV show in New York on March 26th 1967.

Clapton used the guitar exclusively onstage and also recording the *Disraeli Gears* and *Wheel's of Fire* albums with it, and was also featured being interviewed and demonstrating the guitar's capabilities in the *Cream Farewell Concert* VHS tape and DVD. At the actual farewell concert, though, he used a Gibson Firebird for the first house, and a semi-acoustic Gibson ES 335 for the second show and although for selfish reasons I had secretly hoped he would use the SG, Clapton was right in not doing so as the world had turned a page by that time and the hippie era the guitar had represented so perfectly had practically burned itself out by then.

The last time he played and recorded with this Iconic SG was for Apple recording artiste, Jackie Lomax, on a single and album track titled *Sour Milk Sea*. Clapton left the guitar at the Apple studios in George Harrison's care, who in turn loaned it to Lomax. In 1971, at a recording session at Mink Hollow Road studios in Woodstock, New York, Lomax worked and became friends with Todd Rundgren, who expressed an interest in the legendary guitar. Rightly or wrongly but nevertheless hard-up, Lomax sold it to Rundgren for $500 on the understanding he could buy the guitar back at a later date for the same price.

A year went by and Lomax hadn't returned with the $500, so Rundgren had the somewhat deteriorating paintwork and the guitar as a whole, refurbished. Now, quite rightly, regarding himself as the owner and calling it 'Sunny' in respect of Cream's *Sunshine Of Your Love* song, Rundgren sold the guitar in 2000 at a Southeby's silent auction for $150,000. The anonymous buyer then sold it a few years later to an unknown collector, for $500,000.

Alan Burridge at The Bourne Beat Bar, Bournemouth
With his replica 'The Fool' SG Guitar

Recently, the Vintage Guitars Company have produced replicas of Clapton's 'The Fool' SG guitar and as the hand painted art is bespoke for every instrument, each are fittingly also a unique re-creation of that iconic one-of-a-kind instrument. The only differences from Clapton's original is that the 6-pointed stars are painted with the usual 5 points and the wood sprite isn't holding the triangle or the spoon-shaped beater, but other than that, it's a stunning piece of Rock art.

Elias Hulk.

School friends, James Haines, bass, and Grenville Fraser, rhythm guitar, and an un-named drummer, started out as a band named 'Free Love' playing festival gigs around Europe as a soul covers band. The drummer was replaced by another local sticks man, Bernie James, and in 1969 they were joined by lead vocalist, Pete Thorpe, and gigged as The Harvey Wells Soul Band. They were from the Westbourne and Boscombe areas of Bournemouth, close enough to make rehearsals and picking one another up in the van for the gigs easily manageable.

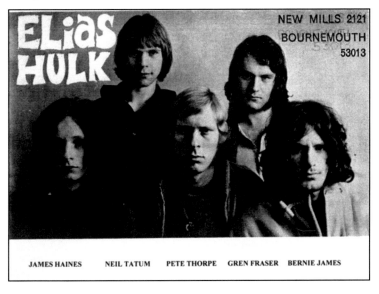

JAMES HAINES   NEIL TATUM   PETE THORPE   GREN FRASER   BERNIE JAMES

103

Then, guitarist Bill Napier joined, but soon left due to family commitments and he was replaced by Neil Tatum, who hailed from Derby. They won a residency at Bournemouth's Pavilion Ballrooms, and also played endless one-nighters around the UK supporting bands like Marmalade, Ginger Baker's Air Force, Spooky Tooth, The Nice, Hawkwind and The Small Faces.

Thorpe's place in the band caused them to re-think their strategy, and the addition of vocalist, Neil Tatum, caused them to change their name to Elias Hulk and start rehearsing original 'Progressive Rock' material.

Original Album Cover of *Unchained*
Issued by Young Blood Records in 1970

They decided to spend some time in London and whilst doing the rounds of knocking on record company doors, dropped into the Young Blood Records office, who appeared to be looking for a Progressive Rock band at the time. Young Blood agreed to pay for some demos, so the band went into Strawberry Studios in Manchester in 1970 (with Eric Stewart of The Mindbenders and 10CC) to record some original songs. This led to a full one album contract with Young Blood. Elias Hulk still had a heavy gigging schedule, so the *Unchained* album was recorded virtually live in about two days. It was released featuring the tracks: *We Can Fly / Nightmare / Been Around Too Long / Yesterday's Trip / Anthology Of Dreams / Free / Delhi Blues and Ain't Got You.*

Reissued Album Cover of *Unchained*
Beat Goes On (BGO) Records in 2007

The album made the Charts in Germany and sold modestly elsewhere. Pete and Grenville left to join Creed, and Phil Clough came in to replace them.

Elias Hulk played regularly at The Pavilion, had a residency at The Temple in Wardour Street in London and also supported The Alan Bown Set, Trapeze and The Groundhogs on their travels.

Now highly regarded and much sought-after amongst progressive rock enthusiasts (original Young Blood label vinyl copies have changed hands for £750!) the *Unchained* album has since been re-released on the obscure Korean or Japanese Airmail label in the 1990s, by Astro Zombie in 2000, See For Miles in 2002, and remastered and posthumously re-released on CD on BGO Records in 2007.

In March 2008, Gren, James, Phil and Bernie got together at the Listen Inn Studios, near Shaftesbury in Dorset, to record a 3 track CD EP titled *Unfinished Business* on their own label, the sarcastically named Old Blood Records, which has also been distributed by BGO Records. The tracks are as powerful and enjoyable as those on *Unchained*, and the band have lost none of their magic over the 40 years between the two sessions. This current line-up does not dispel the chance that they may play a few gigs at some point.

Room.

Despite being runners up in The Melody Maker 'Battle of the Bands' competition in 1969, the somewhat disappointed members of Room were then both surprised and thrilled when they too were awarded a recording contract with Deram Records. Their constant gigging on the circuit and regular rehearsals in between times had brought them to a peak of performance and after just a day in Decca's West Hampstead studio in the Summer of 1970, they had completed and delivered the *Pre-Flight* album.

Pre-Flight was and still is an ambitious blend of classical, rock, jazz and blues. Critically well received at the time of release, it didn't, however, break the band into mainstream commercial success. Their only recording, *Pre-Flight* was remastered and re-released on CD in April 2008 on Esoteric Records.

Tracks: *Pre-Flight Parts 1 & 2 / Where Did I Go Wrong? / No Warmth In My Life / Big John Blues / Andromeda / War / Cemetery Junction Parts 1 & 2.*

Musicians: Jane Kevern (vocals and tambourine), Roy Putt (bass guitar and album sleeve artwork), Bob Jenkins (drums, congas and percussion), Steve Edge (lead and rhythm guitars), Chris Williams (lead guitar).

Hailing from Blandford and despite their phenomenal gigging schedule they were, unfortunately, yet another one of the late '60s bands who recorded an amazing album only to disappear without a trace. (See the listings at the back of the book and web-site roomprogressive.blogspot. com).

Room
Chris Williams, Jane Kevern, Roy Putt, Steve Edge, Bob Jenkins

Everyone but everyone who followed the bands playing the vibrant Bournemouth scene during the 1968 to 1971 era could not fail to have seen Room supporting one or more of the visiting main attractions. Other than playing virtually every rock and pub venue in Dorset and beyond, Room are one of the few bands who gained a support residency at The Ritz. They were unique in their music, and the rock fraternity of Bournemouth and Dorset as a whole were very proud of their achievements and behind them all the way throughout their career.

And they were no strangers to the London scene either, playing The Marquee, The Revolution Club, The Temple and Klook's Kleek amongst others, along with no less than a Royal Albert Hall appearance in January 1971 supporting Pentangle and Fairfield Parlour.

And despite the 40 years since its recording, *Pre-Flight* has stood the test of time, and has lived on to be a very sought-after album of Primal Prog-Rock.

Note: *Bassist, Roy Putt, went on to play with several Bournemouth-based bands, notably Raw Deal, Mission Impossible, and lately The Jim Etherington Band.

*Lead guitarist, Chris Williams, was in The Average Blues Band, and 'made an honest woman of' (vocalist) Jane (Kevern); they are now the grandparents of three kids.

*Steve Edge gave up performing after leaving Room, but continues to play guitar, mandolin and the Irish bouzouki.

*Bob Jenkins has played on some high-profile sessions, as well as drumming with B-Sharpe.

*There would be no chance of the band reforming.

Yes.

On the strength of their performance at The Royal Albert Hall as co-support band, with Taste, at Cream's Farewell Show and buying their first *Yes* LP and probably the 1970s *Time And A Word* as well, Yes' Winter Gardens show on March 10th 1971 was something of a must. No I hadn't gone Prog Rock crazy but their excellent guitarist Steve Howe, who has forgotten more about playing a guitar than I ever knew, had played *The Clap* at the Royal Albert Hall with the amazing Mason Williams' *Classical Gas* tune integrated within it. The track was on the *The Yes Album* which this tour was promoting (but not with *Classical Gas* as this would have created song-writing and copyright problems) and I wanted to hear it played live again.

Of course, a few other Yes tracks had become favourites in the meantime, *Yours Is No Disgrace* from this new album being one of them. Although The Winter Gardens gig was pretty good, *The Clap*, or just *Clap* as it was credited on the LP sleeve, was a disappointment to me as without *Classical Gas* in there sparking it up, it had simply lost its impact and I came away disappointed.

A bit of a harsh judgement, perhaps, but my heart was in guitars, and it had only been Steve Howe's mastery of *Classical Gas*, which I didn't think I would ever see or hear anyone play that well live, which captured my interest. So, despite *Yours Is No Disgrace* still being a favourite, Yes and their Prog Rock were not really my pint of lager and lime.

The Faces & Thin Lizzy.

The Small Faces had lost their guitarist / vocalist Steve Marriott (1947-1991) to the supergroup he formed with The Herd's Peter Frampton, and Spooky Tooth's Greg Ridley (1947-2003) which they named Humble Pie. So the remaining musicians recruited Ronnie Wood on guitar and Rod Stewart on vocals, both having worked together in The Jeff Beck Group. But Wood and Stewart were taller characters, so the band decided to drop the 'Small' part of the name and move forward as The Faces. Completing the line-up would be original members Ronnie Lane on bass, Ian McLagen on keyboards, and Kenney Jones on drums, and together they would play the Boscombe Ballrooms on October 8th, 1971, with Thin Lizzy as support.

By this time, The Faces had released their *First Step* LP in 1970 and their hit single *Maybe I'm Amazed* and were promoting their soon-to-be-released *Stay With Me* single and second album *Long Player*.

And they were everything we expected of them, even with Kevin's 'Uncle Rod' strutting his stuff onstage as only he does. But although they were guitar driven, I was still hurting from the loss of my 'Big 3' favourite bands. It was no fault of The Faces as my friends loved them to bits, but I was looking for a more guitar-driven band than they were or ever would be.

However, Eric was and always will be 'the complete' Small Faces and The Faces fan, and he remembers quite vividly the excellent slide guitar solo Ronny Wood played at this particular gig so it *was* my hurting which was, perhaps, masking my outright enjoyment. But there again, we can't all like every group, can we?

The Thin Lizzy we would see as support band that evening, who were plugging their first self-titled *Thin Lizzy* Decca album, despite being the Phil Lynott (vocals and bass), Eric Bell (guitars) and Brian Downey (drums), wouldn't fill that void within me, either.

It was quite some awe-inspiring (and breathtaking sight) to see Phil Lynott (1949-1986) up there, centre stage. Dark skinned, with a wild 'Afro' hair-do and drainpipe jeans, he was quite something to see, even at that point. Much like other 'great' stars, Lynott had the charisma and charm to grab an audience and did so from the start to the finish of the gig. And if you'd care to check the gig listings herein, Lizzy were no strangers to Bournemouth even at this early stage in their career; they were a *working* band, with every intention within them of making it to the top. Also, at this point in their career,

STARKERS
Royal Ballrooms, Bournemouth

Mel Bush presents

The Faces

with **Thin Lizzy**

and
Cochise

FRIDAY 8th OCTOBER

8pm to 11.30pm

BAR

Tickets : 95p Advance £1 Doors

Advance Tkts from : Setchfields Records 95 Old Christchurch Road
Shapes 14 Richmond Hill, Bal Tabarin, The Coffee Shop Christchurch
Enquires - Bournemouth 65356

Poster for The Faces, Thin Lizzy Concert
Starkers, Royal Ballrooms, Boscombe on 8th October 1971
Courtesy of the Bourne Beat Bar, Bournemouth

Lizzy had yet to achieve their success, (which they did, 2 years later in 1973) with the single that broke them through to wide acclaim and an appearance on *Top of the Pops* with their superb *Whiskey In The Jar* single.

Privileged as we were to see this comparatively rare Thin Lizzy line-up, I was still hurting from losing, one way or another, my teenage heroes and I would be very hard to please in trying to find a replacement. Don't get me wrong, The Faces and Thin Lizzy were great, but they didn't have what took me years to deduce what I was missing, the *volume* or the *crunch* in their music that I had lost with the demise of my 'Big 3' in The Who, Cream and Hendrix.

And much like Wishbone Ash and Whitesnake (whom we had or would be seeing at The Winter Gardens and Portsmouth Guildhall), I couldn't get my head around the dual lead guitar line-ups where the guitarists were playing in unison / against one another. This way of playing guitar was far too contrived for my personal taste, I preferred the unrehearsed guitar solos rather than each player knowing and copying every note the other played.

As a short interlude from the main story here, we watched Whitesnake (the Bernie Marsden / Mickey Moody line-up) at Portsmouth's Guildhall, supporting (I think) Lynyrd Skynyrd (or perhaps they were headlining, I can't remember) and we were seated downstairs under the balcony and the guitars clashed like they were being played inside a huge bell and sounded awful! Sadly, despite the rest of the world loving them, I could never get my head around any of the dual lead guitar line-ups. And before anyone jumps in to wave the twin guitar Motorhead line up in my face, Phil Campbell and Wurzel *never* played in unison à la Thin Lizzy, Wishbone Ash or Whitesnake, yet somehow Lynyrd Skynyrd with *three* guitarists managed to do so, admirably, without any clashes. Also within this, the twin-guitar line-ups played contrived / previously worked out guitar routines, whereas I prefer the spontaneity of the one-guitar solo and the fact that it is 'different' each time it's played. But Thin Lizzy's guitarists have also had their solo moments under the spotlight, and Brian Robertson particularly gave his all for *Still In Love With You* on the 1978 *Live And Dangerous* album.

Pink Floyd.

Their most famous and what would become one of the top 3 Best Selling Albums of All Time in *Dark Side Of The Moon*, started out from quite humble beginnings in the South of England in January 1972. Not actually released until 14 months later, Pink Floyd were of the mind to try out their ideas for the proposed album on the road.

With the original working title of *Eclipse*, the Floyd made their 'first attempt' at playing the album live onstage at The Dome in Brighton on January 20th 1972. It didn't work out quite as well as expected, but according to www.pinkfloyd.co.uk the 'first complete performance' took place the following evening at Portsmouth Guildhall. Their show at Bournemouth's Winter Gardens on the 22nd would also allow privileged fans to bear witness to this extremely early presentation of what would become one of rock's greatest and most significant works ever and Southampton's Guildhall crowd would also share the same page in Rock History the following night.

Released those 14 months later in the UK on March 24th, 1973 and with the title changed from the formative *Eclipse* to *Dark Side Of The Moon*, the rest as they say is indeed history, as the album spent almost 29 years in America's Billboard Charts and has sold in excess of 40 million copies worldwide.

The Groundhogs.

The Groundhogs had visited Bournemouth before and gigged at The Ritz in their earlier days. Somehow though, as we had to be selective since we couldn't afford to go to every gig we would have wished to, I didn't see them live until they toured and played the Winter Gardens in 1972 with their No.8 chart LP *Who Will Save The World? The Mighty Groundhogs.*

In my collection I had (thanks to Terry Best, who is a massive Blues enthusiast and had played me the albums) *Blues Obituary* from 1969, the No.9 album from May 1970 (which was a huge favourite with pal, Alan Plummer, as well) *Thank Christ For The Bomb, Split* from March 1971 and this current album, which was released in an absolutely splendid 'comic book art' gatefold sleeve depicting The Groundhogs with the Tony McPhee (guitar), Pete Cruickshank (bass) and Ken Pustelnik (drums) line up, doing as it said they would on the cover, saving the world!

And although every album by The Groundogs is (and even those released since are included in this comment) a classic, there had been none more so than this one to that particular date, due to two of the 8 fine tracks being *Amazing Grace*, which as a Rock version is knockout and the exceptional *Bog Roll Blues*. We had also found a particular place of fondness in our hearts for their *Cherry Red* track on the *Split* album and, as a whole, The Groundhogs have never released one duff track.

Their Winter Gardens show was loud, but 3-piece bands had to be that way, and amplification (thanks, mainly, to The Who's Pete Townshend's close work with Jim Marshall at Marshall Amplification) had moved forwards in massive leaps and bounds. I'm not sure about the other two members of the band, but in keeping with the *Who Will Save The World?* album theme, Tony (TS) McPhee wore a black, Batman-like cape throughout the show. Some of the songs (as virtually *every* rock band at this time had followed Cream's example) would be transformed from their original three or four minute LP track length into massive, 20 minutes or so long guitar solos, which were fine if you were stoned or drunk, but maybe a little tedious if you were straight. But somehow, on this particular occasion anyway, the sound wasn't too good and the McPhee solos didn't grab the attention, and although there's no way I could have stood onstage like TS and played anything like him, the boredom aspect put me off The Groundhogs for quite a few years. But there again, if I'd hit the booze a little harder and taken along a joint, I known damned well I wouldn't have just written that last sentence.

However and today's kids will laugh at this, dope wasn't easy to get hold at the time and I personally didn't actually get the chance to try it until 1984. Another thing was, in the 1960s and 1970s, none of the people I mixed with were even interested in giving it a try; never mind going through the (reputed) dark and murky underworld in an effort to try and get some, so it was a mixture of friends not doing it, and being unable to get hold of the stuff.

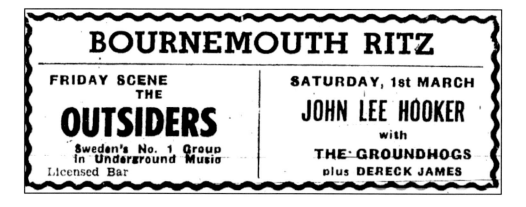

BOURNEMOUTH RITZ

FRIDAY SCENE	SATURDAY, 1st MARCH
THE	
OUTSIDERS	**JOHN LEE HOOKER**
Sweden's No. 1 Group in Underground Music	with
Licensed Bar	**THE GROUNDHOGS**
	plus **DERECK JAMES**

The Roundhouse Cave Bar.

However, sidetracking slightly but sticking with dope, The Cave Bar beneath The Roundhouse Hotel at The Lansdowne in Bournemouth at the time would perhaps have been the place to get it? Going there, as soon as you walked in the door the air was so thick with smoke you were almost stoned by the time you reached the bar to order a drink. My second visit was exactly the same, but a fight broke out between a biker and some pencil-up-his-ass Mod twat who was doing far too much mouthing off and he ended up with the palm of his hand cut wide open on a smashed pint beer glass. One of the other bikers frogmarched him around the entire floor area of The Cave Bar, a bit like a trophy, insinuating "don't fuck with us or you'll end up like this!" His left hand, still pouring with blood, happened to 'flop' onto the back of this chick's white jumper; a ruckus ensued and the remaining Mods who were quite leery with booze started goading the bikers even more to try and reclaim their lost credibility over the situation. Someone called the police and as soon as the sirens were heard, the place cleared as quickly as if someone had dropped a rancid fart. Personally, I detest any argument, confrontation or fight situation and have no time for it, so I was out of there when I saw the friction from the Mods brewing. The Cave Bar was an OK place, but was, I believe, a complete den of iniquity for the Bournemouth drug scene at the time. Perhaps if I had mixed with a different crowd I would have fitted in, but seeing the state of some of them and great looking as some of the girls obviously were, I'm sure they'd have been so out of it they wouldn't have remembered who you were or where they'd pulled you, or indeed how you'd performed between the sheets by next morning, anyway.

Perhaps we didn't try hard enough to get hold of and try some drugs?

Perhaps we weren't brave enough to want to try them, anyway?

Perhaps I wouldn't be here to write this had I delved deeper?

Perhaps some of my friends from the time wouldn't be here, either?

A young chap we'd known at school had already died after walking off an apartment balcony three floors up whilst on an LSD trip.

Perhaps that had put us off?

We couldn't have afforded rehab!

But they didn't have rehab at the time, so you just stayed a junkie, or died!

Whatever!

We're still here to tell the tale, and this tale needed telling.

Status Quo. (again!)

The Bournemouth suburb of Boscombe had a venue in the 70s called The Royal Ballrooms, also known as 'Starkers', when local impresario Mel Bush promoted concerts there. Built in the Victorian era, the building has all the grandiose splendour associated with anything regarded as 'Royal', including a sweeping, semi-circular stairway to take you upstairs to the seated arena. These days it is known as The Opera House.

Like the other venues in and around the town of Bournemouth, the Ballrooms had also cottoned on to the fact that this 'Pop music fad' wasn't going to go away and the younger generation adored it, so there was money to be made.

So, you recall my earlier story about Status Quo's performance when they were 'Mods' at The Ritz? Right. Well, with *Ma Kelly's Greasy Spoon* released in 1970 and *Dog Of Two Head* released in 1971, Quo had dispensed with their 'Mod' image and those Psychedelic Pop tunes had grown their hair and become a Progressive Rock band, and had continued in that vein with their 1972 album, titled *Piledriver* and all three are still, for me anyway, excellent albums.

Do you remember the power cuts of the 1970's? In an effort to force the issue in getting a pay rise, the Electricity Board were plunging the towns and cities of the UK into instant darkness and didn't tell anyone when they were going to do it. It proved a point, because without electricity everything grinds to a halt and becomes extremely cold and dark.

Bearing in mind how disappointing Quo had been at The Ritz, well, it couldn't happen twice, could it? Hmm. Well, it did.

Once again, the crowd at the Ballrooms, much like that at The

Ritz, consisted of about 50 to 60 people and the Quo boys looked extremely upset at this poor turn-out as they walked around the dance floor, then around the seated area, with scowls on their faces as if to say, "is this gig really worth bothering with?"

When they walked onstage, Mike (or was he Francis by this time?) Rossi went to the microphone and said, "They tell us the power might be low tonight (referring to the electricity strikes) so we're gonna turn everything up!"

Well, it was L-O-U-D LOUD!

But we had heard LOUD before with…

AC/DC.

At The Village Bowl and The Who at The Pavilion, so if Status Quo wanted to be pedantic, then let them get on with it.

Every band, thank goodness, *can* see more than they often let on from the stage. Fortunately, a rather a good 'walk up' crowd arrived and Quo noticed the venue filling up to make for a better audience which gradually brightened the band's mood. So, as their mood improved, so too did the music, and the volume became more reasonable as the audience, as they tend to, deadened the sound somewhat merely by being present (as their clothing and bodies absorb some of the sound) and a much better gig was enjoyed by everyone.

Had it not been for those three, what were regarded as 'Progressive Rock' albums, Quo would have been, I'm sure, just a 5-minute one-hit-wonder and wouldn't have followed on to be the international stars they are today!

Note: Every band pre-sells a certain amount of tickets before the day of the show, what is termed as the 'walk-up' are tickets bought on the day or evening of the show, by punter's who decide, right at the last minute, to go along. So often, what appears to be a poorly sold gig can often lead on to be almost sold out by the 'walk-up' crowd.

Led Zeppelin.

But the Status Quo gig and the band's moodiness had not impressed my then girlfriend (now my wife) but I would go on to redress this minor blip in our total of excellent local concerts by getting us both a ticket from, strangely enough, WH Smiths book shop in Poole High Street (as for some odd reason they were the local ticket agent) for another show at the Ballrooms later in 1971. The tickets were for a band whom a great many younger local rock fans still do not believe would have bothered to get out of bed for a gig in a South Coast town, like Bournemouth, but yes, they did, and they were…*Led Zeppelin!*

Yes indeed, Led Zeppelin played Boscombe's Royal Ballrooms, on December 2nd 1971 and believe me, there were so many people in the audience, they were, as they say, literally hanging from the rafters. (This was a 'Starkers' gig and local promoter Mel Bush had a great deal to do with booking the bands playing the venue, so this is probably how we came to get this exceptional gig!)

You read it right the first time: Led Zeppelin: Jimmy Page, Robert Plant, John Paul Jones and John Bonham (1948-1980) actually trod the boards and played a gig at the Boscombe Royal 'Starkers' Ballrooms!

And in a word, they were magnificent!

They were on tour plugging the *Led Zeppelin III* album, and Robert Plant hit those high-pitched notes right at the beginning of *The Immigrant Song* with ease and precision and then told us when they came back for their first encore that they were all suffering from the 'flu!

That's professionalism for you!

Listening to the *Led Zeppelin* album in the record booth in Setchfields, thinking, "Well, they're supposed to be The New Yardbirds, but they're nothing like them, really," is quite a fond memory. Suffice to say everyone who attended walked out of the Ballroom feeling twenty feet tall and elated that they had experienced one of, if not THE best gig of their lifetime!

Some friends saw Robert Plant driving around Boscombe in a Range Rover pre-gig, which is a nice little anecdote, and since then, most of the fans and locals who attended the show have had quite a job convincing others that Zeppelin actually played the Starkers Ballrooms in 1971. Indeed, after writing a review of the Zeppelin tribute band, Whole Lotta Led for the Mr. Kyps local (Parkstone) live venue website after their appearance in December 2005 and mentioning this Boscombe show, a punter at the venue, as I was, for another show at a later date, approached me and shook my hand. "Thanks for verifying that Led Zeppelin played Boscombe in your review," he said, with a huge smile on his face, "I've been telling people for years, but no one believed me, now with your review *I've got the proof!*"

And indeed, even at the time *Led Zeppelin III* was released, already the band was far too big for the likes of Boscombe ballrooms, but there you go; *it happened* and I feel sure it would be the Mel Bush connection that made it possible and Mel's the man we had to thank. All I can add is, those of us who had a ticket and went along were extremely lucky!

Dave Robinson of the BourneBeat Bar supplied a set list for the December 2nd Led Zeppelin 'Starkers' Boscombe show:- *Immigrant Song / Heartbreaker / Black Dog / Since I've Been Loving You / Stairway To Heaven / Going To California / That's The Way / Tangerine / Bron-Y-Aur Stomp / Dazed And Confused / What Is And What Should Never Be / Rock 'N' Roll / Whole Lotta Love* medley including *Bottle Up And Go, Heartbeat, Hello Mary Lou, Lawdy Miss Clawdy, I Can't Quit You Baby / Communication Breakdown* including *Turn On Your Love Light / Weekend / It'll Be Me.*

Van Der Graff Generator.

During 1971, Van Der Graff Generator were touring their 3rd and for me most memorable album *H To He, Who Am The Only One*, and I went along with Terry Best and his girlfriend, Jeanne, to Boscombe's

Royal Ballrooms to see them. A strange title for an LP, yet one which the more out-and-out 'Progressive Rock' fans would enjoy for singer / guitarist Peter Hammill's quirky titles and poetry / lyrics.

John and Tony Smith in association with Tony Stratton Smith and Terry King present TOGETHER IN CONCERT

VAN DER GRAAF
GENERATOR
LINDISFARNE
GENESIS

Saturday, 13th February at 7.30pm
ADMISSION : ALL SEATS 6/- (30np)
Numbered tickets available in advance from the box office

WINTER GARDENS · BOURNEMOUTH
Exeter Road   Telephone 26446

Poster for Van Der Graff Generator, Lindisfarne, Genesis Concert
Winter Gardens, Bournemouth on 13th February 1971
Courtesy of the Bourne Beat Bar, Bournemouth

To say the crowd at the Ballrooms was sparse would be an understatement, with probably only 45 to 50 people who became even more barely noticeable within the expanse of the venue. People were sitting, with one fan even lying on the floor in front of the stage to watch the band play, laid-back or what? But give them their due, VDGG gave the performance their very heart and soul, as every band should, as if the place was packed to the rafters. They were professional right the way through their set, right down to the eight-and-a-half minute song from this album, *Killer*, which was about a shark and went on through rock history to become their signature tune. VDGG were great and I enjoyed the gig, but they were just a bit too jazzy for my taste. However, our local King Crimson guitar hero, Robert Fripp was guest on the album for the *Emperor In His War Room* track, which keeps the local connection intact.

Curved Air.

In 1971, pioneering British Progressive Rock band, Curved Air, after gaining recognition for their first single, *It Happened Today*, went on to have a hit with their second, titled *Back Street Luv*, which achieved No.4 in the UK charts. The band had gained prominence with their first album, *Air Conditioning* which was also notable as the second picture disc album ever to be released. With their show-stopping *Vivaldi* track featuring their gifted violinist, Darryl Way, Curved Air was most certainly in the public eye.

Sonja Kristina of Curved Air

Their second album, titled simply *Curved Air*, also had the *Back Street Luv* single as one of the tracks, which gave them the credibility of not being one-hit-wonders and sealed their rock icon status. And great and 'different' as they were with this talented violinist within their ranks, Curved Air's greatest asset was their vocalist, Sonja Kristina as there were very few if any other females on the then current rock scene, never mind one so attractive and alluring. So when they paid a visit to the Winter Gardens in either 1971 or 1972 whilst riding their then current and well-deserved fame, we went along, not only to enjoy the music, but also for the sheer carnal lust of seeing Sonja live onstage. And here am I admitting it, but I bet there are scores of blokes who felt the same way and claimed they attended "for the music, man, we wanna see 'em play *Vivaldi*."

Yes, it played a huge part in the scheme of things, but we had been idolising blokes in bands for years but now we had a top-notch female and she was so much easier to worship than a bloke. In hot pants, flowered, hippie-styled suede boots and copious amounts of ostrich feathers, Sonja was the 'Rock Chic' we had been waiting for years to see (with perhaps only Marsha Hunt, Julie Driscoll and Christine Perfect preceding her.)

Still on the scene today with her MASK project, Sonja Kristina, (born Sonja Kristina Linwood), is still the attractive woman she was in her 20s and her music is equally mature and enjoyable and should not be ignored.

Rock Circus.

Around 1972, the local 'Pub Rock' gigging scene came to life again with one band in particular making local prominence Rock Circus. These guys knew what they were doing by breathing new life into the old Buddy Holly, Eddie Cochran et al classics and playing them around the local circuit. They achieved quite a following playing: The Halfway Hotel (now re-named The Grasshopper) in Bournemouth Road, Parkstone; The Potter's Arms in Hamworthy,

The Shipwrights Arms on New Quay (now demolished), The Old Harry (now The Globe Café) in Poole High Street amongst other venues. Fans would follow them and go to every possible gig they could but then suddenly, and for whatever reasons, they simply disappeared from the scene. This was such a pity, but these days that fabulous era is still brought to life by local bands such as Rockin' The Joint, who play the Mr. Kyps venue in Parkstone on a monthly basis.

**The Grasshopper (Halfway Hotel)
Parkstone**

**The Globe Café (The Old Harry)
Poole**

**The Lighthouse (Arts Centre)
Poole**

**The George Hotel
Poole**

Some of Poole's great rock venues

Team Dokus.

TEAM DOKUS
Management: J. C. THEATRICAL AGENCY
Winchester House,
Maiden Street, Weymouth.
Tel.: Weymouth 4588 or 3233

Left to Right: Terry Lowe – bass guitar, Fred Fry – lead guitar
Steve Hall – twin lead guitar, Phil Bridge – keyboards
Roy Stockley – drums, Roger Hope – vocals.

The Old Harry was a great Poole High Street music venue now re-named 'The Globe' (presumably after the 10 foot diameter, 40 ton Portland stone globe in Swanage, rather than the swashbuckling and heroic Poole pirate, Harry Paye?). On Friday June 2nd 1972 Team Dokus, the band from out-in-the-sticks Shapwick, near Spetisbury in Dorset, played the venue. With their name a light-hearted amalgamation of the F1 racing 'Team Lotus' and 'The Topper' comic character 'Dopey Dokus' the band had won a good following of local fans.

Team Dokus had won the Southern Area Heat and Final for the *Melody Maker* music paper's National Rock & Folk Contest and on the following day would be travelling to London to battle it out with similar winners from around the UK. The prizes on offer were a management deal *and* an appearance on BBC 2's *The Old Grey Whistle Test*. Team Dokus were using The Old Harry as a final rehearsal for the 'Battle of the Bands' contest.

With two guitarists sharing rhythm and lead in Fred Fry and Steve Hall, Team Dokus made up their 6-man line-up with Terry Lowe on bass guitar, Phil Bridle on keyboards, Roy Stockley on drums and Roger Hope on lead vocals.

Drummer, Roy Stockley, had been a pupil of Lytchett Minster Secondary Modern School in my brother's year. Rob had often mentioned Roy practicing his drumming skills with a pair of sticks he brought to school every day 'using the desk tops as his drums'. Roy still has the warm and friendly smile he's always had for everyone and like many of his peers, cycled in to school from Lytchett Matravers every day on his bike, which had the 'cow-horn' handlebars he was very proud of.

I met up with him again after school and pre-Team Dokus when he worked for Wyatts, the local builders. In my guitar making days, I visited Wyatts timber yard off Dorchester Road in Upton to try and buy a piece of wood suitable for a guitar neck and body and spoke to Roy about the project. He didn't have any wood as I wanted it and recommended buying a guitar rather than making it as 'they are difficult to get just right!' Despite Roy's advice, I was too skint to buy one and went on to make several but he was right, because getting the strings to lay right in relation to the fret board, which is known as 'the action', was indeed the most difficult job of all.

But Jane and I attended the June 2nd Team Dokus gig at The Old Harry and hidden beneath my jacket (I can't think why as the band wouldn't have objected) I had an original Phillips cassette recorder, the first personal cassette recorder on the market, which I had bought second-hand somewhere. With a dodgy C120 (1 hour each side) cassette in the deck (they didn't recommend them as the tape was very thin) I recorded Team Dokus' 2 one-hour sets.

One of the main local 'progressive' bands of the day, they played a mixture of cover versions and their own material and began with one of their own songs *Here's Hoping*, then Joe South's / Deep Purple's *Hush*, another of their own with *Feel A Little Higher*, Status Quo's *In My Chair*, Johnny Winter's *Rock 'n' Roll Hoochie Coo*, Fleetwood Mac's *Shake Your Money Maker*, then two of their own compositions with *It's On The Rise* and *I'll Be Waiting Here*, Deep Purple's *Black Night*, John Kongos's *He's Gonna Step On You Again*, Canned Heat's *World In A Jug* and their own *Gut Rock*.

In the second set they played their own *Magic Castle*, Ten Year's After's *Hear Me Calling*, another band composition with *Tomorrow May Not Come*, Wishbone Ash's *Blind Eye*, Deep Purple's *Blood Sucker*, then *He's Gonna Step On You Again* (again), The Savoy Brown Blues Band's *Train To Nowhere*, Black Sabbath's *Black Sabbath* and *Gut Rock* again, which, I believe, was going to be their main featured song at the London play-off.

Some Internet gig listings have highlighted three Team Dokus dates for February 1971: on the 1st at Oakdale Boy's Club in Poole, on the 4th at 'Venue Unknown' in Shapwick, (probably The Anchor At Shapwick pub) and another on the 6th at RAF Abingdon, so that's proof, if any was needed, that this band were well and truly on the gigging map and more is the pity they didn't win that *Melody Maker* contest, after which they became disillusioned and split up.

Meeting with Roy at The Chequers pub in Lytchett Matravers when he played drums with The Beachcombers, I told him about the cassette of their Old Harry gig. He was thrilled and borrowed it and made a copy for each member of the band. Now, I often think about playing it to reminisce about those great times, but then decide not to as the tape would probably disintegrate.

However, Team Dokus, as our photo shows, had a couple of professional recording sessions, so they were on the path to 'making the big time'.

The first session for a proposed EP took place at Wessex Studios in London on February 15th, 1971, when they recorded *Feel A Little*

128

Higher / I Feel Her Fire / Tomorrow May Not Come / My Name Is Death.

At a second session, they recorded 2 tracks which were taken from recordings made over 2 Saturdays on October 9th and 16th, 1971 at Regent Sound Studios at Denmark Street, London, for a proposed album. *Tomorrow May Not Come* would have been the A-side and *Fifty Million Megaton Sunset* would have been on the flip.

Album Cover of *Tales From The Underground*

The *Fifty Million Megaton Sunset* track somehow made it from acetate onto *The Psychedelic Salvage Co. Vol.2* LP and CD, as well as onto both the *Psychedelia Vol.3* LP and *Hen's Teeth Vol.3* CD compilation albums.

In 1994, Tenth Planet Records released an LP, and later a CD of the Team Dokus album under the title of *Tales From The Underground.*

The release was made using recordings taken from studio acetates of the proposed original album.

Tracks Side 1: *Fifty Million Megaton Sunset / Night Of The Living Dead / Here's Hoping / On The Way Down*.

Tracks Side 2: *Visions / Tomorrow May Not Come / Big Red Beast / I Can't Wait / Feel Your Fire / Fifty Million Megaton Sunset (reprise)*.

Tales From The Underground, although Team Dokus would have chosen a different title, was a concept album based on how life might be after a post-World War III nuclear holocaust.

Natural Gas.

Another local band playing the local pub circuit were Natural Gas, who we first happened to see at The Old Harry, which for us, was fast becoming a favourite haunt. But often, if we didn't like the band of the evening, we would move on to The George, The Shipwrights or The Potters Arms to see if anyone more to our taste was playing. The Poole, Hamworthy and Parkstone music scene was thriving in the early 1970s as so many young people had watched other musicians make their fortune and they wanted to try and do the same.

Natural Gas were among the contenders, playing covers of other band's songs rather than their own material. They had a singer who thought he was Mick Jagger (nothing wrong with that and he also had the lips from what I remember), a long blonde haired / bearded guitarist who owned about the first ever Gibson SG guitar I'd seen up close and a dark-haired and moustached bass player who sang back-up vocals. We had watched and enjoyed them on a Friday or Saturday evening at their Old Harry gig and then, much to our surprise in the office Jane and I worked in at the time in Market Street in Poole, the photocopier broke down and who should pay a visit to repair it - Natural Gas' bassist, who introduced himself as Barrington Beeston. Whilst repairing the machine, he cajoled us into promising we would go along to their next gig the following

Saturday at the Sir Walter Tyrell pub near The Rufus Stone in the New Forest.

They played songs like Crazy Elephant's *Gimme, Gimme Good Loving*, Joe South / Deep Purple's *Hush*, and quite a few Stones songs to keep their Jagger-like singer in seventh-heaven mimicking his hero. The band travelled to the gig in an ex-Post Office Morris Minor van and after they had set up Barrington sat down with us. I asked him where the singer was. "Oh, he's gone off to Swanage to try and find us some chicks!" Of course, 'Mick Jagger' didn't return, so Barrington took over on vocals and then added afterwards, "It's not unusual, he often does this!"

The Pink Fairies & Russell Hunter.

Pink Fairies drummer Russell Hunter, was born in Woking Surrey, but when he was two and a half years old his family relocated to Poole in Dorset, as his father worked for BDH (British Drug Houses), a London-based industrial chemical company who were moving their premises to West Quay Road in Poole. As an incentive for their key staff to move with them, BDH had accommodation built, mainly in roads off Moorland Way in nearby Upton.

Hunter grew up in the area and attended Upton Infant's School, then Lytchett Minster Primary and began his drumming career after meeting Robert Fripp (who was later to be King Crimson's leading light) at Wimborne Grammar School upon passing his 11+ exams.

One of his first bands was The Dictators, but he only lasted one gig and then moved on to The Big Six Beat Combo and then The Hurricanes, who played Motown, Chuck Berry, Bob Dylan, The Searchers and Beatle's songs. They later had a name-change to The Mob, who supported the top visiting bands like The Yardbirds and The Animals; they also backed Jimmy Reed. They then toured the working men's club circuit in the North-East playing Teenage Beat Nights.

The Mob later went into a recording studio with (*Telstar*) Joe Meek as producer, and recorded a single which sold few copies. Russell then left the band and worked at Bournemouth Post Office for 3 months or so. But as he had left The Mob, a young Greg Lake joined them, changed their name to The Shame and released their *Don't Go Away Little Girl* single on MGM Records.

Hunter was more interested in Rock 'n' Roll and wanted to go and live in London where both the people and the nightlife was more interesting and bands could achieve some degree of success. He passed a Civil Service exam and in doing so was transferred to work at Her Majesty's Stationary Office in London in 1965. Moving around the big city scene during his leisure time, he quickly found clubs like UFO and Middle Earth and by 1967 had met Mick Farren who had a band named The Deviants. Russell drummed on The Deviants' albums titled *Ptoof, Disposable and Deviants 3*.

The Deviants fell apart during a North American tour, sacking Farren and from the wreckage of the band The Pink Fairies were born. Hunter went on to drum on the Fairies first album, 1971's *Never Never Land*, along with numerous other assorted LPs throughout the band's rather un-together history.

Released in 2008, one of the finest Pink Fairies albums featuring Russell Hunter is *Finland Freakout 1971* for which he co-wrote the liner notes. The album was recorded by the Finnish Broadcasting Company at the Ruisrock Festival, Turku, Finland on Saturday August 21st 1971.

Uriah Heep & Lee Kerslake.

Despite many appearances in the Bournemouth venues, a Uriah Heep concert eluded me probably on the grounds of budget versus other bands playing in the area at the same time and only being able to afford tickets for those most favoured. Nevertheless, Jane was a big fan of their *The Magician's Birthday* and *Demon's And Wizard's* albums, not only because they were and still are superb albums on their own merit, but also for another local musician in their ranks.

Drummer Lee Kerslake, was born in Bournemouth and at first, along with Greg Lake, joined The Gods. Lake quickly left the band, but Kerslake stayed on with the nucleus of the musicians who were The Gods, and later, in 1971, to become Uriah Heep. Lee's first album with them was in fact *Demons & Wizards* in 1972 but he left them in October 1979 and then joined again in April 1982.

Lee Kerslake's career spans scores of albums by: The Gods, Head Machine, National Head Band, Toe Fat, Uriah Heep, Ken Hensley's and David Byron's solo work, Ozzy Osbourne and Living Loud. However, in early 2007 it was announced on Uriah Keep's website that he had left the band due to ongoing health problems.

Mugwump.

A band named Mugwump appeared at The Old Harry around this time, too. A covers band, they played a cross-section of rock from Deep Purple, Black Sabbath and so on. But one Saturday, girlfriend Jane and I were watching them, with a deathly response from all the other patrons in the pub might I add (we applauded every song) when for the first time as far as I was concerned, Mugwump played Led Zeppelin's *Stairway To Heaven*, which I had never witnessed covered by any band before and they did it perfectly.

During the interval between their two sets, the guys in Mugwump came over with their beers and sat with us, more out of appreciation for our clapping than anything else and I asked them, "Don't you get disappointed when there is so little response from an audience?" The singer replied, "We don't worry about it, we get paid regardless, but we watch the punter's feet and if we see they're tapping them or moving them around, then we know the music is getting through." This was a good point and any up-and-coming bands might like to bear this in mind, should they ever play to a similarly 'wooden' and unresponsive audience!

Abel Cain.

This band would play The Potter's Arms in Hamworthy on a fairly frequent basis, as did many others whom I have unfortunately forgotten their names. But this four-piece, much like Team Dokus, had actually written some of their own songs and among them was quite a fast-paced and self-titled track titled *Abel Cain*.

The Potter's was an excellent venue, with the stage set immediately to the right as you walked through the front door into the public bar. The pub is still there today and I have fond memories of the bands and the good times we had watching them there when sitting in the traffic queue outside, waiting for Poole's lifting bridge to open.

The Potters Arms, Hamworthy

The League Table, The End of The Ritz, and The Birth of The Hive.

Other than within the fairytale world of banal and sickly-sweet TV programmes like *X-Factor* in the real world, even today, bands and artistes have to go through their apprenticeship and in so doing pay their dues before climbing to a higher division in the league table. Well, divisions in a football league table are the only way I can think of to explain the ladder bands climb in the world of Rock 'n' Roll.

Division 4 is the spit and sawdust pubs and working men's / ex-service men's clubs where you might get chairs, bottles, and glasses thrown and if you didn't know before, you learn about how to control a crowd. Thin Lizzy's Phil Lynott was a master at crowd control, perhaps a little too much so. Phil insisted his band knew *every* Thin Lizzy song and, by and large, there would be no actual set list, per se. Phil would read the crowd reaction and listen for the tracks they called for, so in the event, the crowd dictated the songs, but it made for a wide and varied set.

The Ritz Ballroom
1969

Division 3 would be the clubs like The Ritz, a step up from division 4 but still a place where crowd control is a key word as they're right there in front of you. By this time the band would be professional, touring regularly and with a record contract and an album to plug.

Division 2 bands would be playing venues like The Winter Gardens, Poole Arts Centre and suchlike. The album would have seen a fair to middling placing in the charts and the record buying punters would have increased to fill the need to book the larger capacity venues such as this. At this point, although there would have been one or two roadies before, now with more equipment, lights etc., several would be the norm. Elevated on a larger stage with a gap between the apron and the crowd, security would be provided by the venue.

The Hive (formerly The Ritz)

Division 1 is in the class of Wembley Arena, Madison Square Gardens and suchlike and the bands are in the World Class Entertainment arena where several *thousand* fans want to see the band / artiste as hundreds of thousands of albums have been sold. By now, both band and venue security is tighter than the proverbial gnats' backside and unless they are very careful the band can become sealed within a bubble where reality is something from the past not remembered particularly well. Although of hallowed status, that grip on reality should be strived for and achieved otherwise the slide back down to division 4 happens all too quickly when the band get fed up with playing much the same set every night, begin arguing and then split up; this is generally described in the press as 'irreconcilable musical differences'

As bands and artistes achieve these greater levels of success, the venues like The Ritz would begin losing their clientele as we, the punters, followed our bands to those larger venues like The Winter Gardens. Likewise, as our generation moved onwards with our music, so too The Ritz had to change to ensure survival by catering for the changing tastes of the younger 'Disco' generation. It did so, altering its name to The Hive Disco. It is interesting to note how in October 1972, a very young Thin Lizzy played the venue as The Hive Disco, probably as one of the last live rock bands to play there as they had been booked prior to the name-change. (In 1983, The Ritz / The Hive would be demolished to make way for the massive Bournemouth International Centre entertainment complex, known as the BIC).

Barclay James Harvest.

They were / are a bunch of talented hippie musicians who play emotionally charged, if on occasion somewhat depressing rock music, and on October 27th, 1976 they would play The Winter Gardens and stir those emotions within us whilst promoting their magnificent *Octoberon* album. They provided some of the best stereo effects we had heard to that date, notably with the combined beauty and sadness of the *Suicide?* the final track on this LP. The end of the almost 8 minute song re-creates the previous lyrics in fantastic sound-images of a man walking upstairs to a roof and being pushed (?) off and the audio effects of the wind rushing past his ears as he falls to ground gives the track an uncanny and quite frightening reality. The first time I heard this (on headphones) the man hitting the ground made me jump!

Barclay James Harvest's music is extremely moving and a great many of their albums have been bought and enjoyed immensely but in the live arena like The Winter Gardens, they would play, we would applaud, then they would play and we would applaud and so on for 90 minutes and then they left the stage and I thought, *blimey, if they hadn't moved to play their instruments, they wouldn't have moved at all.* And that's they way they were / are; it might as well have been four cardboard cut-outs onstage with their LP playing through the PA system. But that's just my opinion. Musically, BJH are unsurpassable, they play anthemic, majestic, British rock music which stirs incredible feelings of emotion no other band has ever stirred before and quite different to the adrenaline rush but they were very boring to watch.

Band personnel: John Lees (guitar and vocals), Les Holroyd (bass, keyboards, vocals), Stuart 'Woolly' Wolstenholme (keyboards / vocals / guitar), Mel Pritchard ([1948-2004] drums / percussion).

Blue Oyster Cult.

If you stopped anyone over 45 years old in the street and said the words, "Blue Oyster Cult," they would probably reply, "Don't Fear The Reaper," by response. And despite other odd hit singles and an album or two here and there *Don't Fear The Reaper* is their signature tune and the reason why we would go to see them at The Winter Gardens on June 3rd, 1978.

From the USA, Blue Oyster Cult were out on tour plugging their *Spectres* LP and we were fortunate in having them visit the South Coast.

What other songs they played other than *The Reaper* I can't remember but what I do remember is the most fabulous and amazing laser light show of my entire life! In some ways, perhaps, it's the wrong thing to be remembered for, as it should be the music first and

Poster for Barclay James Harvest Concert
Winter Gardens, Bournemouth on 11th May 1976
Courtesy of the Bourne Beat Bar, Bournemouth

foremost. Yes, I bought a few of their LP's either before or after the event and enjoyed them, and also had the 12" single of *The Reaper* whilst still looking for a replacement for the loss of my 'Big 3', and Blue Oyster Cult would not be it despite this stunning show.

One member of the band had a laser ring or something in his hand, which he pointed at flash-bombs on either side of the stage to set them off. They had a laser light, probably in front of the drum riser, which beamed a flat light rather like a wafer the width of the Winter Gardens, which was really weird as it came up to eye level when you could actually look across the top of it. They also had a revolving mirror-ball fixed into the roof, which had dozens of laser lights beamed onto it most of the time and as the rays of light bounced off you felt you had to duck or they'd hit you. No, I wasn't 'on' anything, this was how it happened and probably more besides that I don't remember. And knowing myself as I do, I was always reluctant to try any kinds of drugs because I know I would like them, they would have cost me money I didn't have with a young family, and addiction or death would have followed.

So, yes, Blue Oyster Cult provided the show of a lifetime as far as the visual side of Rock 'n' Roll was concerned with their laser light show; others like Motorhead would provide different types of 'wow factor' lighting in the future, though.

As a footnote, Andy Perkins also attended this gig. I'd become friends with him after Jane and I worked with his then girlfriend, (later, his wife) Karen at Waitrose in Westbourne. We would also bump into one another and ended up with record collecting (and darts) as our common ground at a rather good 50s and 60s oldies vinyl shop named Back Track Records, which used to be in Southbourne. Andy was a huge fan of the original Bill Haley / Buddy Holly Rock 'n' Roll and Blue Oyster Cult. Whenever we meet, he reminds me how I got him into Jimi Hendrix by giving him a spare copy of the *Voodoo Chile (Slight Return)* 45; quite how I had a 'spare' copy escapes me.

Poster for Blue Oyster Cult, Japan Concert
Winter Gardens, Bournemouth on 3rd June 1978
Courtesy of the Bourne Beat Bar, Bournemouth

Dire Straits.

On April 10th 1978, Eric, Alan Plummer and I went to the Arts Centre to see The Climax Blues Band, who'd had a hit single with *Couldn't Get It Right* in 1976. Unfortunately, they couldn't get it right *again,* because they had Dire Straits (who are they, we wondered?) as their support band on this Autumn UK tour. Perhaps we had read something about them in the music papers, I can't remember, but even so, words cannot be converted into music, so they were probably quite a surprise to everyone?

Dire Straits were on the tour to plug their first, and at the time still unreleased *Dire Straits* LP. Well, if you can remember the first time you ever heard *Sultans Of Swing,* or indeed any of the other tracks on that album and the effect it had on you, then you might understand how blown away we were watching them play live! For me, Mark Knopfler's finger-picking style played within the rock format was breathtaking, I had never witnessed anything quite like it before, and he was almost as exciting, but in a different sort of way, as seeing Jimi Hendrix live for the first time. I cannot say he *was* as exciting as watching Jimi Hendrix, but he is still up there as one of the most sensational guitarists I have ever watched - wow!

To be honest, Climax Blues Band should have cancelled the tour because following Dire Straits was an impossible task and Straits quite simply 'blew them off the stage'. The entire Arts Centre crowd appeared to be in some odd state of delirium after being completely bewitched by Dire Straits as a band, and Knopfler as a guitarist. No one could wait for the album to be released, Dire Straits music was just so unique and completely different to anything else at that point in time, it was simply a 'must have' LP. Although we would never be party to 'musical snobbery', we have always had the privilege of being able to say, "We saw them when they were an up-and-coming support band."

But seeing them as that lowly support band in the Wessex Hall at the Arts Centre (it was a theatre gig, not stand-up) it made it more than apparent that they were going to be big very fast and of course, they were, and that first album went on to sell something like 15 million copies worldwide, never mind the phenomenally successful singles and LPs that would follow. Climax Blues Band were brave taking Dire Straits on tour with them, because they just *could not* follow an act like that and, to be fair, there were not many bands around at the time who could have done so.

The Punk Era.

Married and with a young family by now, going to see bands had taken a backward step, even though buying an LP on a reasonably frequent basis wasn't. Jon Kremer's Westbourne Exchange & Mart had moved on from selling used electrical goods, as had the public from buying them (mass production had made them cheap and throwaway) and his shop still nestled within the frontage of The Grand Cinema at Westbourne had been re-named Bus Stop Records simply because there's a bus stop right outside the shop door and Jon sold nothing but LPs, singles, cassettes and VHS video. Lately, with the advent of CD and DVD, its name has changed to Bus Stop Discs.

As record buyers we also had been given another string to our bow when Mickey Tarrant opened Armadillo Records about half a mile away in Queens Road, right on the border of Bournemouth and Westbourne, not that it bothered the ever-affable Jon, as he knew the guy anyway as he had started out being a customer. As ever with our mutual lunacy, Eric and I would have our nickname for it of 'I'm A Dildo', as we did silly things like that just for a laugh, and quips like, "Did you go down dildo Saturday?" would spring from it as part of our Monday morning work conversation.

Mickey, who ran the shop with another guy as a business partner, catered in general for the Punk enthusiast. (Mickey was also the man behind the Midnight Express venue, who brought bands like The Cure, Blancmange and The Smiths to our town from March 1982 to New Year's Eve 1983.)

As ever to the avid record collector, the Armadillo Record shop was a cornucopia of fabulous LPs by The Sex Pistols, Blondie, Television, The New York Dolls, Motorhead, The Damned, The Buzzcocks, Siouxsie and the Banshees, The Clash, The Ramones; you name 'em, they had 'em. A great shop to visit, and 'different' from Bus Stop as much of this 'Punk Music' had yet to achieve 2nd hand status and thereby wouldn't be on sale there for a few months.

Usually on the Saturday following pay day, we would have a 'family outing', (well, more like me being selfish, actually, as I had to have a pay day treat or I regarded it as not worth going to work and I would buy a couple of 2nd hand LPs!) to the a-little-bit-further-away-town of Christchurch where, just over the railway bridge on the left hand side was Snupeas Records owned and run by a guy named Terry. He had also been a previous customer of Jon at Bus Stop (indeed, what serious local record collector hadn't?) and much like Armadillo, Snupeas catered mainly for the Punk fans. Snupeas can now be found in Boscombe, still selling records and CDs, but under a different ownership.

The Punk Era not only introduced the (better sound quality of the) 12″ single, it also introduced 'Limited Edition' and 'shaped picture discs' to the record collecting world. But considering Punks as a whole were not generally supposed to be wealthy people, it seemed odd to me as they wouldn't have been able to have afforded buying them? But the theory was this, if these different pressings were released side-by-side with a regular 7″ single release, when the fans bought two or more of the different formats (e.g. on occasion it was possible for the record companies to release a 7″ single, a 12″ single, a picture disc and a cassette single with everything but the 7″ being a Limited Edition, often with the additional lure of different 'not-released-elsewhere' tracks being on the various formats) it sold, depending on how many formats it was released in: two, three or four times the amount of records and would thus achieve a much better chart position. So, this was common practice at the time and many of these 'unusual' and Limited Edition releases quickly became

144

rare and worth far more than their original value and Snupeas specialised in them and had quite a few rare gems displayed on the walls and hanging from the ceiling.

Once you got to know Terry, which wasn't difficult as he was a likeable and friendly character, you'd be thumbing through the albums and he'd walk over and offer you his car key whispering, "It's the (whatever make his car was) over the road, go and have a look in the boot." I would leave Jane and the kids, toddlers as they were, in the shop, whilst I nipped over to Terry's car and opened up the boot, which would be choc-a-bloc with vinyl bootleg LPs.

There would literally be *everything* by *everyone* who was anything and anyone on the Punk scene, from Blondie to Siouxsie and the Banshees and Elvis Costello to The Stranglers and everyone else in between. Live concerts were the bootlegger's forte, but 'studio outtakes' were also a favourite and I found and bought a double LP of *Blondie Live At The Glasgow Apollo*, paid £15 for it, arrived home, looked inside the 'Want Ads' in *Sounds* (weekly music paper, where I remembered seeing someone after a copy in the Small Ads), then wrote to the guy, who was happy to pay £35 + postage for it and made myself a few quid! That was the only time I was ever lucky with a scoop like that, and it had been a gamble as they guy might have had it offered by someone else and then I'd have had to find another home for it! But I feel sure I would have sold it eventually, yet as it was, I was pleased at making a few extra quid, which knowing me was probably spent on the kids instead of buying *more LPs.*

Whether you liked Punk Rock or not, every self respecting music fan owned a copy of *Never Mind The Bollocks* by The Sex Pistols, because essentially *it is* a Rock album; it was The Pistols clothes, attitude and their audience that made it 'Punk!' But the extra keen fan who would end up being the 'cool dude' amongst his friends, would also own a copy of their *Spunk* bootleg LP. The fairly local Wimborne Market had a bootleg stall at the time and after being tipped off by Eric I found a copy there. It had much the same tracks as *Bollocks* but they were 'different studio takes' which The Pistols had recorded for their short-lived (a few days, wasn't it?) contract with A & M Records. Some, or dare I say *all*, of those 'takes' were / are far better than those on the actual *Never Mind The Bollocks* LP as far as most aficionados are concerned and "The Sex Pistols don't get much better than this!" as one reviewer succinctly put it, carried within it the message of the masses. Strangely, well maybe not, because despite it being bootlegged someone had to own the original tapes, *Spunk* was given an official CD release in 2006 and has been trendily 'expanded' to offer 15 tracks now and sells quite brazenly in these more modern times under the title of *The Original Spunk Bootleg* and is available for about £5!

The Tubes.

Played Poole Arts Centre at some point during 1979 on their 'Remote Control World Tour' and although the show was enjoyable, it proved 'Theatrical Rock' wasn't for me. People walking around the stage dressed as Marlboro cigarettes and another as the packet wasn't really my kind of entertainment and although songs like *White Punks On Dope* will always be classic, I keep their *Young And Rich* album mainly for the ultra-erotic *Don't Touch Me There* song. They played this during their Poole set and both the male and the female vocals and the 'tongue-in-cheek' horny lyrics, plus the 'Big Production' sound, for me, make it one of my all-time Top 10 favourite tracks.

Kate Bush - Tragedy at Poole Arts Centre.

Kate Bush immediately became a megastar after the success of her *Wuthering Heights* single, and was the first woman to have a No.1 hit with a self-written song. After the *Kick Inside* and *Lionheart* albums, she decided to tour, with the 'warm-up gig' chosen to be at Poole Arts Centre on April 2nd, 1979.

The venue has a 'bowled' auditorium where the seated audience looks down upon the stage, but the radical Arts Centre also has the provision for a 'flat floor' to be fitted over the top of it for the more rock-driven acts. The Kate Bush show, like hundreds of others, was played as a 'flat floor' gig. Somehow, after the show, Ms Bush's lighting director, 21 year-old Bill Duffield, slipped or tripped and fell into the chasm below the 'flat floor'. He was taken to Poole Hospital where he later died. Devastated as Ms Bush and the members of the band and crew were, they continued with the tour, using their Hammersmith Odeon date on April 12th as a Benefit Concert for Bill Duffield. Ms Bush has never toured on the live circuit since and it is down to speculation whether this is due to Duffield's accident, her penchant for perfection, which she felt she could not achieve 'in concert' or a mixture of the two.

'The Old Grey Whistle Test' & 'Sight And Sound In Concert'.

'Whispering' Bob Harris, whose catchphrase was 'nice', hosted BBC 2's rock and alternative music TV show *The Old Grey Whistle Test* from 1971 to 1978. Preceding it, BBC 2 had broadcast *Sight & Sound In Concert*, whereby a concert would be broadcast on TV (now in colour and almost every home had one) with the option of turning the TV sound down and tuning your hi-fi system VHF radio in to Radio 1 to hear the same concert being broadcast, in stereo, to match the pictures on-screen. This was quite a radical innovation and for rock fans it was a definite 'must tune in' most weeks as the featured bands were generally rather good. (AC/DC's incredible performance, from London's Hippodrome in 1977, was released on DVD in 2008 and is an excellent parallel of their Bournemouth gigs of that era.)

So, *The Old Grey Whistle Test* as well as catering for 'the old hippies', of which my generation were a now a part, with bands like Lynyrd Skynyrd, (who always won the 'New Year's Eve Phone In' for the video of their amazing *Free Bird* song), Rory Gallagher, ZZ Top (with their knockout videos) and so on, Whispering Bob Harris also catered for the Punk audience with appearances by The Police, The Stranglers, The Adverts, Radio Stars, The Pretenders, Elvis Costello etc. With a very young family and just one wage coming in instead of two, the opportunity of going to a gig was still there but wasn't as easily affordable as it had once been. So it was ideal to watch *The Whistle Test* to find out about anything or anyone new on the scene or if any of the featured bands might be worth going to see if their tour came this way and it also became a good talking point at work.

By now, I worked with Eric in a hardware warehouse behind The Old Thatch pub, on the Uddens Industrial Estate, near Ferndown, and either he or our mutual colleague, Tony Munch, would tape three quarters of John Peel's 2 hour evening radio show on a C90 cassette, probably once or twice a week, and play it through the warehouse PA System. The PA was there so that Jackie, on reception, could call any one of us to the phone, whilst at other times it had the radio playing through it. So, for 90 minutes during the day we would have the Radio 1 *John Peel Show* playing through the warehouse. And Peel played a lot of Punk, in fact, it was largely due the records he played between 10pm and midnight that the whole Punk movement became so popular and a great many of those bands who went on to achieve fame and fortune can attribute their success to John Peel and his 5 nights a week radio broadcast. Also championing Reggae music and popularising it in the UK, Peel was largely responsible for Althea & Donna's *Uptown Top Ranking* No.1 hit single in February 1978. Likewise, he brought out the best of the 'pub rock' bands, with Dr. Feelgood and, again, Ian Drury (1942-2000) & The Blockheads achieved a No.1 with *Hit Me With Your Rhythm Stick* and also The Motors with *Airport* even though their *Dancing The Night Away* was and still is a personal favourite.

So we would hear Peel's (sometimes) weird and wonderful and (now and again) completely off-the-wall selections, from *Teenage Kicks* by The Undertones to *I Could Puke All Over You* by White Boy on the Diddley-Squat record label and then on one of these tapes of his show, he played *The Train Kept A Rollin'* by Motorhead. More than familiar with The Yardbirds version, this one by Motorhead sounded *amazing!*

We asked Jackie on reception to rewind the tape so that we could listen to it again, yes, right, knockout! So the following Saturday I drove the family straight to Armadillo Records, where I'd noticed the Motorhead 12" single *and* the Motorhead LP, and bought them both!

So had Eric and our main daily talking point became Motorhead, and, "Why is it we keep playing their records, but don't get fed up with hearing them?"

Motorhead.

They had been called 'The Worst Band In The World' and also had a growing reputation for being extremely LOUD!

Loud!

Right! Yes!

At some point, Eric, Alan Plummer and I had been to see AC/DC at The Village Bowl in Bournemouth. With Bon Scott (1946-1980) and Angus Young fronting the band, they were an absolute joy and a privilege to watch and good grief, they were effing LOUD! Long, wide and low (like a massive letter box) as a gutted out ex-ten-pin bowling alley was, with their complete Hammersmith Odeon backline and PA in place, it was an experience something like having your head stuffed inside one of Concorde's engines. In fact, we actually walked *behind* the band's PA to watch them, where it was (very) marginally quieter and we were so thrilled at seeing them, yet the volume was absolutely ear-shattering in those low yet wide confines.

Eric's memories of these two AC/DC gigs are: "Went the first time with (Alan) Plummer, there were only about 50 of us. It was so loud it made you feel ill. I can still remember to this day the intro to *High Voltage*, in fact I think I can still hear it!"

Note: AC/DC played The Village Bowl twice, once on their 'Dirty Deeds Done Dirt Cheap' UK Tour on February 28th, 1977 and again on May 23rd 1978 on the 'Powerage' UK Tour.

Irrespective of Bon Scott's death, I am surprised AC/DC didn't tick all the boxes in replacing my 'Big 3'. AC/DC as a band at that time were the ultimate LOUD scuzzy rebels, with gaping holes in Bon's jeans almost with his balls hanging out and at one point he spat a hocker of phlegm over drummer Phil Rudd's head, hitting the backdrop; they were the ultimate in crashing chords and screaming guitar solos. But had AC/DC done the (dirty) deed for me, they wouldn't have after Bon's passing, because although the music was and is just the same, Brian Johnson as their vocalist has never sat comfortably in my book. But my book doesn't matter, there are *millions* of AC/DC fans out there who just kept on loving the band and still do but for me Bon epitomised everything the band were about and he and Angus were the perfect onstage partners and that's something Angus and Brian, for me anyway, have never achieved.

Onward…

The Village Bowl had previously been known as The Bournemouth Hard Rock and Motorhead had played there on August 26th 1975 as one of their very first dates. Somehow, probably due to the usual lack of finance, we didn't get to see them for that show but after our AC/DC experience and Motorhead's reputation as The Loudest Band In The World needed checking out, Eric and I attended the Motorhead gig at the Poole Arts Centre on October 22nd 1978. *We had* survived AC/DC and believed no one else would even be in the running as far as LOUDness was concerned.

In a word - WRONG!

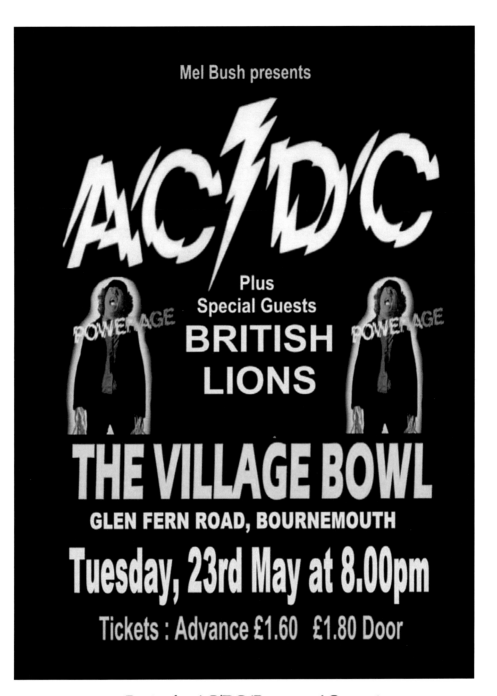

Poster for AC/DC 'Powerage' Concert
The Village Bowl, Bournemouth on 23th May 1978
Courtesy of the Bourne Beat Bar, Bournemouth

The Motorhead set was a lengthier version of their *What's Words Worth* live LP, and coupled with Lemmy's quite outrageous (at the time) onstage banter, they were, as far as I was concerned, just what I had been missing since 1970 when my 'Big 3' disappeared. And after peeling ourselves from the Art's Centre's Wessex Hall walls and dusting our stupidly gibbering selves off to go home, I had a smile on my face as wide as wide could be for the remainder of my lifetime as I had found The Who, Cream and Jimi Hendrix wrapped up inside this one, amazing, three-man band called Motorhead.

And we would see them again the following April at Portsmouth's Guildhall on their 'Overkill' tour just to make sure we hadn't got it wrong. And, no, we hadn't, so when they played their 'Bomber' UK tour (with an amazing lighting rig shaped like a Second World War German Heinkel HE 111 Bomber, which took everyone's breath away) the following Autumn, we went to their shows at Bracknell, Bristol, Southampton and finally, also taking our wives to the Bournemouth Winter Gardens show on December 8th, 1979 *just to make extra sure.*

And as far as I was concerned, although I still listen to and go and see other bands across the spectrum, Motorhead had filled the void left when my teenage heroes' either died, split up and / or moved on to other things I wasn't so keen on, although, in fairness, The Who redeemed themselves with one or two of their latter-day songs like the magnificent *Won't Get Fooled Again, Who Are You?* and *Baba O'Reilly.*

Fortunately, we are all extremely different in our tastes, and no two record collections, even between a brother and a sister, will ever be the same, and for that fantastic human individuality we must be grateful.

So Lemmy Kilmister and Motorhead seemed to answer all the questions in my life and still do. They struck a chord, literally, and waved a banner that I could identify with and wanted to follow through right to the end, one way or another.

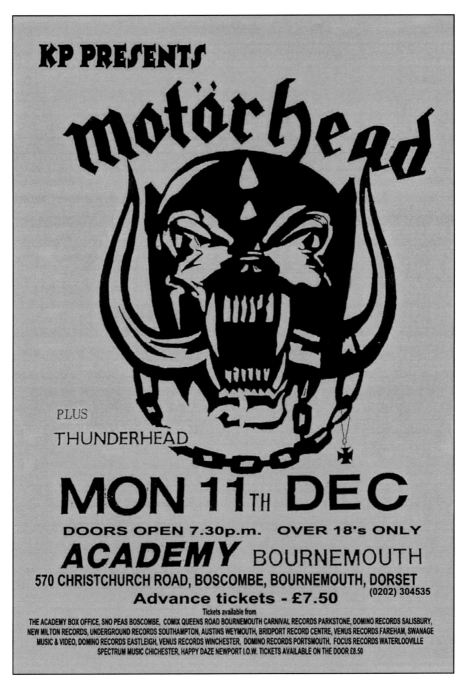

Poster for Motorhead Concert
The Academy (The Opera House), Boscombe on 11th December 1989
Courtesy of the Bourne Beat Bar, Bournemouth

Vinyl LP's, CD and Downloads.

We were reluctant to move on from our trusty vinyl LPs into the new world of the compact disc when they elbowed their way into the record shops in October 1982. Most of us regarded this new recording medium with extreme distaste and that the only benefit that it could possibly offer was that the only major downside to the 12" LP sleeve was that it would become constantly and annoyingly 'bent' in the record shop racks and that facet had been eliminated.

But our vinyl LPs, despite getting easily scratched and being a 'static magnet' for dust and fluff, seemed to have a more dynamic and 'earthy' sound about them which the sterile perfection of the CD could neither imitate nor provide, a bass-end and a depth which we all noticed was missing. But for the younger generations, the CD was and still is more user-friendly and the record companies endeared us old vinyl addicts by re-releasing all those long-deleted albums they swore they had lost the master tapes for, by cleaning up the original recordings and adding bonus tracks of the relevant singles, and live tracks, or previously unreleased material, and even stuff the bands hadn't even originally intended releasing as they regarded it as substandard.

So we became swayed towards CD but most still kept the vinyl and the wherewithal to play it but can we endear ourselves to this new fangled thing called The Download? No! We Jolly Well Can't!

A large part of buying an LP (usually in a Setchfield's bag) or even a CD was bringing it home on the bus under your arm, getting indoors, removing it from the sleeve, (and getting a lovely whiff of the virgin vinyl – Hmmm!), putting it on the turntable, placing the needle in the groove and hearing the crackles and then the joy and delight of hearing the first song! And whilst we sat there listening, we would be having a good look and a read of the LP sleeve which was always a must.

CD wasn't quite so captivating or endearing as we had lost the 12" square artwork on the sleeve for a start but nevertheless at least we had the artwork and usually a nice little booklet to read.

So, what has a 'download' got on offer other than the song?

Zero! Sweet Nothing!

The LP and the CD will gradually die out as we surely will do, and the download generations of the future will miss out on that tactility, that pleasure in owning something and having it on a shelf or in a rack to get out and look at and play when we so wish. The download generations will have nothing like that, but there again, today's music is about as unimportant and disposable as downloads themselves, so I rest my case.

The Adrenaline Rush.

With drugs everywhere in our world, be they legal or illegal, most people fail to notice or even take the time to enjoy the most natural drug our body produces: adrenaline.

Adrenaline is the product of excitement, for those likeminded reading this book, it is generated from the moment our favourite band or artiste announces a UK tour. It further escalates when we find out there is a gig in or around our home town. Although only at a minor level, the adrenaline buzz accelerates slightly when we buy a ticket for the show, it is in our hands, and the reality of being there for a legendary performance hits.

But we are owner of that ticket and come hell or high water *we are going to that gig!* In recent years tickets can be on sale in February or March for a show the following Autumn, and when friends say, "I see so-and-so are playing the BIC." We can immediately reply, "Yeah! And I've got my ticket already!"

This adds to the escalating adrenaline buzz and as the weeks or months pass by it hides within our psyche until perhaps we feel a bit down or depressed and then the thought of that show and that we are the owner of a ticket to see it lifts us with the gentle release of a few more of those adrenaline endorphins.

This continues until the week of the gig and the excitement

escalates even more as we are so near yet so far, and the days seem to drag their heels as if begrudging our forthcoming joy.

Some fans have the day off work to visit the venue. Just seeing the juggernauts outside and watching the road crew wheeling in the sound and lighting gear is a thrill. Perhaps during the mid-afternoon when the band's coach arrives, a glimpse of our heroes might be captured, or if we're very fortunate and can get close enough, a "Hello," a handshake, an autograph or perhaps all three? (A photo with the band or a Backstage Pass are of course every Rock fan's dream and the latter often but a once-in-a-lifetime occurrence – unless you're a female wearing high-heels, fishnets and a mini-skirt and then the world is your oyster, just as long as you're happy to follow it through to the next morning when he says, "Bye!" and closes the hotel room door behind you as you leave.)

But enough of all that, the band are there and some fans like to stand outside the venue to hear them play their sound check. This pumps the adrenaline again as they are playing it to you and just a few others who have had the same idea and not the concert hall filled with people. The sound check can be the source of almost the ultimate adrenaline buzz, especially if the band plays a song which isn't in that evening's set or is a tune completely off-the-wall for that band in particular.

When the doors open for the concert itself, the adrenaline starts building upon entry to the venue. Just to be a part of the evening, the gig and the tour and being surrounded by all those like-minded people escalates the whole feeling and the stall selling the T-shirts definitely clicks the endorphins further into gear.

The support band or bands are either heard as a muffled roar of noise from the bar or if they are any good, a casual look from the rear of the venue. It's the Main Attraction, the Bill Toppers we paid our money to see and if the support bands are crap, the time drags relentlessly. But when the lights go down and silhouettes appear onstage lurching around in the dim light of a roadie's torch, the bar has emptied and *everyone is there* to see them, then the adrenaline surge is pure magic. When the first chord of that familiar and favourite anthem is played, adrenaline overdrive is within sight.

The following 90 minutes pass by like a flash and we wish they did likewise when we're at work and all the time the adrenaline is pumping, we're applauding, we're jumping up and down and then … they're gone.

Make a lot of noise! Clapping, stamping of feet, cheering, get them back for the encore! The adrenaline rush hits overdrive for the encore, two or perhaps three songs, the final chords then, soaked in sweat and bowing to us in thanks of being a great audience, they really are gone.

But that buzz will be with us going home, the adrenaline rush will stop us sleeping when we get to bed and the volume will be an irritating yet familiar and comforting sound like an aircraft jet-engine in your ears but at least you got your money's worth, especially if it lasts for a couple of days or so.

And just like the lyrics David Gates wrote called *The Guitar Man* for his band, Bread, the band go on to the next venue, the next gig, the next city, the next audience, the next country, the next tour, the next sweat-soaked crowd applauding them, onward ever more on the Rock 'n' Roll circuit of the world.

And likewise, we are looking for our next gig, our next ticket to buy, our next adrenaline rush. And when both we and the bands we watched were in our 20s, did we ever imagine they would still be playing and we would still be going to see them when we were in our 50s and 60s?

No, we didn't, but thank goodness we and they are able to carry on doing so, and long may we remain the Rock 'n' Roll rebels we truly are.

The Electric Church.

Jimi Hendrix spoke the words around the time of the *Band Of Gypsies* album and Lemmy Kilmister included them in Motorhead's

On The Road song and those words are - The Electric Church.

Not a great one for practicing religion per-se myself as it expects us to believe in some especially wild and outrageous 'miracles', which even The Archbishop of Canterbury has been known to agree could have been 'conjuring tricks', the Rock concert hall is however, not that far removed from the set-up of the Church.

In much the same way as the religious Believer, we go to the concert venue in the hope of finding and / or receiving messages from our own real living-and-breathing gods via the lyrics of their songs, which can and often are radical and / or thought provoking, or their messages spoken between those songs or indeed in interview.

We are the Congregation, They are The Real Live Gods onstage at the Altar. We worship their every word and utterance, but instead of Hymn Numbers we are given song titles, which Hymns also use, of course but "This is *Ace Of Spades*" goes down rather more comfortably in the Rock venue than "This is Hymn Number 234."

But we go, we worship; often we sing-along with those lyrics en-masse and feed our souls from their spoken and sung words and leave at the end fired with the adrenaline rush and fuelled by the event which enhances and brightens our lives, just as the Religious Believer takes the same facets from the Hymns and Prayers of his Church to fulfil his life, giving him the will to carry on against everything which simply living our lives throws at us.

In essence, they are one and the same: The Church and The Electric Church that is Rock 'n' Roll; we attend, we draw power from our god or gods to help us tread a better path in life than that which we would no doubt tread without their guidance and wisdom. And if the message is perhaps not there from the words and the lyrics, perhaps they are by the way our idol lives his or her life and our own is thus enriched by attending their church, hearing their hymns and those short sermons given between the songs.

In all aspects of life, we human beings need a crutch or belief in *someone* or *something* to get us through from birth to death and thankfully, we have the right of being given the choice of whom we worship.

Every war ever fought from the Holy Wars and before to those still being fought today has been caused by different religions fighting about their beliefs and their gods; occasionally, but rarely, a war has been about politics. The Electric Church is unique in being the greatest form of enjoyment ever and even in those recent two world wars which our fathers and grandfathers had to suffer to give us the world we enjoy today, entertainers like Vera Lynn and The Glenn Miller orchestra were there taking their Electric Church and the accompanying adrenaline rush to the troops, to help them get through the horrors they were forced to endure.

As Lemmy Kilmister has said on many an occasion: "Rock 'n' Roll, it's the only Religion which will *never* let you down!" This statement is absolutely true and extremely astute in its observation. At a rock concert, the whole crowd is there to see and hear the main attraction, unlike team events in sport, there is no opposition present and thus no winning or losing side. In Rock 'n' Roll, *everyone* goes home charged up in a positive way, so everyone *wins*.

Likewise, there are no barriers; people of *any* religion, skin pigmentation or sexual preference can go along and enjoy the performance as a fan of any particular style of music and it gives everyone a common ground of simply being a fan of that genre of music. The whole thing about it is the escapism, be it The Electric Church or The Ethnic Church. That time spent makes us think about something completely different other than our jobs, or our family, or our home life and any problems there may be within any of them. That time away and the complete change in our thought patterns provides the escapism required to refresh us so we return to our lives with a different outlook we are then able to look upon any problems from another perspective and perhaps find they were not as insurmountable as we first believed. Thus, we believe our 'God' has helped us and whichever 'God' one worships, if it provides those answers then it has achieved its aim.

Age, the style of ones hair, or indeed whether one has any hair, tattooed or not, pierced or not, the way the people who are there are dressed just does not matter, all of these what can be seen as barriers in other aspects of our lives make no difference in the rock arena; *we are fans* and that is our common ground, and it is *all* that matters.

A war has never been fought in the name of Rock 'n' Roll…yet!

*   *   *

Every music fan has their own story about the bands and artistes they have seen in their lifetime, some of whom they miss because they're departed and others who are still here and whose records they still collect today. Music has and always will be with me as the Number One in my life and I like almost everything except musicals, opera and freeform jazz, which I just find an awful noise. I enjoy everything else from Elvis Presley and Gene Vincent through to Snow Patrol and Amy Winehouse and most things in between. It's been great writing about some of these bands who were a part of my life onstage for 90 minutes here and there and to applaud those who started out here in the Poole and Bournemouth area for just getting up there and doing it and the few who went on to become famous on the worldwide stage and, in most instances, sold a few million albums along the way.

Circumstance, fate, destiny and a chap named Brian Tawn moved together like pieces of a jigsaw to allow Eric and I to meet Motorhead on their Bomber Tour in 1979 and led to my editing and publishing the *Motorhead Magazine* fanzine until early 1983. Drummer Phil Taylor's family had organized the 'Motorheadbangers Fan Club' over the same period. But when they gave it up Lemmy Kilmister asked for both to be rolled into one and 'Motorheadbangers' continues, despite numerous Internet websites, to be the focal point for Motorhead fans around the world. Now in its 29th year, it has been based in Poole throughout that time.

----o00o--- (__) ---o00o----

Gig Listings:

A fairly comprehensive selection of listings featuring the majority of the Bands and Artistes who played Bournemouth, Boscombe & Poole through the years 1960 to 1980.

Sometime in 1957 - Winter Gardens - Lonnie Donegan & Marty Wilde.

May 11th 1963 - Winter Gardens - Jerry Lee Lewis / Gene Vincent / Heinz Burt / Mickie Most / The Outlaws.

June 21st 1963 - Pavilion Ballroom - Tony Blackburn & The Sabres (with Al Stewart on guitar).

August 4th 1963 - Gaumont Theatre - Gene Vincent.

September 8th 1963 - Gaumont Theatre - Gene Vincent.

September 20th 1963 - Pavilion Ballroom - Steve Marriott & The Moonlites, Zoot Money, Tony Blackburn & The Ravers, Jim Pennel & The Jumpmen.

October 5th 1963 - Le Disque A Go-Go - The Andy Summers' Jazz Quartet.

October 26th 1963 - Gaumont Theatre - Everly Brothers / Bo Diddley / The Rolling Stones - 2 Shows.

October 28th 1963 - Winter Gardens - Dee Dee Sharp / Johnny Kidd / Heinz.

October 28th 1963 - Pavilion Ballroom Beat Club - Joyes & The Boys / Tony Blackburn & The Ravers / Jim Pennel & The Jumpmen.

November 9th 1963 - Winter Gardens - Billy Fury / The Tornados / Joe Brown / Marty Wilde / Karl Denver Trio.

November 16th 1963 - Winter Gardens - The Beatles / The Brook Brothers / Peter Jay & The Jaywalkers / The Vernon Girls / The Kestrels.

November 23rd 1963 - Winter Gardens - The Shirelles / Duane Eddy / Gene Vincent.

December 14th 1963 - Kinson Community Centre - The Dictators.

December 23rd 1963 - Winter Gardens - Gene Vincent.

February 22nd 1964 - Winter Gardens - John Leyton / Mike Sarne / The

Swinging Blue Jeans / The Rolling Stones / Mike Berry / Billie Davis / Jet Harris - 2 Shows.

March 8th 1964 - The Wheelhouse, Poole - The League of Gentleman.

April 15th 1964 - Le Disque A Go-Go - John Mayall's Bluesbreakers

May 2nd 1964 - Herbert Carter School, Hamworthy - Gene Vincent.

May 11th 1964 - Winter Gardens - The Rolling Stones - 2 Shows.

August 23rd 1964 - Gaumont Theatre - The Rolling Stones / The Barron Knights / The Worrying Kind / The Overlanders / The Paramounts / Julie Grant/ Long John Baldry - 2 Shows.

August 30th 1964 - Gaumont Theatre - The Rolling Stones / The Barron Knights / The Worrying Kind / The Overlanders / The Paramounts / Julie Grant / Long John Baldry - 2 Shows.

November 7th 1964 - Winter Gardens - Gene Vincent.

November 28th 1964 - Winter Gardens - Gerry & The Pacemakers / The Kinks / Marianne Faithful / Bobby Shafto / Kim Weston & The Earl Van Dyke Band.

December 31st 1964 - The 45 Club, 45 Poole Road, Westbourne - The Birds, one of The Faces / The Rolling Stone's Ronnie Wood's early bands.

May 15th 1965 - Winter Gardens - The Kinks / The Yardbirds / Jeff & Jon / The Mickey Finn / The Riot Squad.

July 18th 1965 - Gaumont Theatre - 2 Shows at 6.30 and 8.45 - The Rolling Stones, Tommy Quickly & The Remo Four, Steampacket (featuring Long John Baldry, Julie Driscoll and Rod Stewart, backed by Brian Auger's band), Twinkle (backed by Bobby Rio & The Reveilles), The Paramounts (with Gary Brooker - piano, and Robin Trower - guitar, later with Procol Harum, and Trower as a solo guitar star), and John Mayall's Bluesbreakers (with Eric Clapton).

August 2nd 1965 – Gaumont Theatre – Cliff Richard/ The Shadows

October 27th 1965 - Le Disque A Go-Go Club, John Mayall's Bluesbreakers with Eric Clapton.

October 31st 1965 - Winter Gardens - The Searchers / Dionne Warwick / The Zombies / The Isley Brothers.

November 6th 1965 - Winter Gardens - Gene Pitney / The Rockin'

Berries / Peter & Gordon / Lulu.

December 29th 1965 - Le Disque A Go-Go Club - Peter B's Looners (with Peter Green).

June 19th 1966 - Pavilion Theatre - The Small Faces / The Moody Blues / Wayne Fontana / Rog Harrington / The Sean Buckley Set.

August 8th 1966 ? – Pavilion Ballroom - Cream.

August 14th 1966 - Winter Gardens - Tony Rivers & The Castaways.

August ?? 1966 - Winter Gardens - The Walker Brothers / Dave Dee, Dozy, Beaky, Mick & Tich / The Troggs.

September 28th 1966 - Winter Gardens - Dusty Springfield / Dave Berry / Los Bravos / David & Jonathan.

March 17th 1967 - Winter Gardens - The Troggs / David Garrick / The Loot / Normie Rowe & The Playboys / Gene Pitney.

April 1st 1967 - Gaumont Theatre - Roy Orbison / The Small Faces / Jeff Beck / Paul & Barry Ryan / The Settlers / Sonny Childe / Robb Storme. Jeff Beck cancelled and The Creation stepped in.

April 29th 1967 - Winter Gardens - The Walker Brothers / Cat Stevens / The Jimi Hendrix Experience / Special Guest Engelbert Humperdinck / The Californians / The Quotations - 2 Shows.

May 27th 1967 - Winter Gardens - Donovan.

June 20th 1967 - Pavilion Ballroom - Family.

August 27th 1967 - Winter Gardens - The Shadows.

October 12th 1967 - The Ritz - The Move.

November 3rd 1967 - Poole Technical College - The Jeff Beck Group.

November 15th 1967 - Winter Gardens - The Jimi Hendrix Experience / The Move / Pink Floyd / The Nice / Amen Corner / Eire Apparent / Outer Limits.

December 12th 1967 - Royal Ballrooms - Bournemouth Technical College Student's Union Xmas Dance - Traffic.

December 14th 1967 - Pavilion Ballroom - Pink Floyd.

January 16th 1968 - Pavilion Ballroom - The Herd.

March 6th 1968 - The Ritz - Plastic Penny.

April 19th 1968 - The Ritz - The Rock 'n' Roll Revival Show.

April 20th 1968 - Winter Gardens - Gene Pitney / Don Partridge /

Status Quo / Simon Dupree & The Big Sound / Special Guests Amen Corner.

April 23rd 1968 - The Ritz - Jimmy Cliff / Wynder K. Frogg.

April 27th 1968 - Winter Gardens - The Kinks / The Herd / Gary Walker & Rain / Ola & The Janglers / Special Guests The Tremeloes.

May 9th 1968 - The Gaumont - John Mayall's Bluesbreakers with Mick Taylor (Cancelled).

June 16th 1968 - Pavilion Theatre - Scott Walker / Dave Dee, Dozy, Beaky, Mick & Tich / The Rocking Berries.

July 2nd 1968 - Pavilion Ballroom - Bournemouth College Rag Ball '68 - Tim Rose / The Nice.

July 5th 1968 - Pavilion Ballrooms - The Move.

July 12th 1968 - Pavilion Ballroom - Status Quo / The Promise / Rubber Soul.

July 19th 1968 - Pavilion Ballroom - Amen Corner / The Fusion.

July 20th 1968 - The Ritz - Memphis Express.

July 24th 1968 - The Ritz - Fleetwood Mac.

July 26th 1968 - Pavilion Ballroom - Simon Dupree & The Big Sound / Archimedes Principal.

August 2nd 1968 - Pavilion Ballroom - The Pretty Things / Bruce Channel / Dr. Marigold's Prescription.

August 7th 1968 - The Ritz - The Spencer Davis Group.

August 9th 1968 - Pavilion Ballroom - Dave Dee, Dozy, Beaky, Mick & Tich / Lord Maurice / The Balloons.

August 14th 1968 - The Ritz - The Tremeloes.

August 21st 1968 - The Ritz - The Nice.

August 23rd 1968 - Pavilion Ballroom - Amboy Dukes / The Gas / The Fusion.

August 29th 1968 - The Ritz - Fleetwood Mac.

August 30th 1968 - The Ritz - The Perishers.

October 1st 1968 - The Ritz - Fleetwood Mac.

August 30th 1968 - Pavilion Ballroom - The Alan Bown / Lemon Peel / Brothers Bung.

September 12th 1968 - The Ritz - Marmalade (cancelled).

September 15th 1968 - Pavilion Ballroom - Roy Orbison, Jimmy Crawford.

September 18th 1968 - The Ritz - The Nice.

September 15th 1968 - Pavilion Theatre - Roy Orbison / The Jimmy Crawford Four.

September 20th 1968 - The Ritz - Ten Years After.

October 1st 1968 - The Ritz - Peter Green's Fleetwood Mac.

October 4th 1968 - The Ritz - Duster Bennett.

October 5th 1968 - The Ritz - Granny's Intentions.

October 10th 1968 - Pavilion Ballroom - Chicken Shack / Family.

October 12th 1968 - The Ritz - The Rape / Infantes Jubilate (printed as Infantos Jubilatie in *The Echo*).

October 18th 1968 - The Ritz - Simon Dupree and the Big Sound.

October 22nd 1968 - Poole College Fresher's Ball - Spooky Tooth / Elmer Gantry's Velvet Opera.

October 31st 1968 - The Ritz - Junior's Eyes (a John Lodge / Rick Wakeman short- lived psychedelic band).

November 1st 1968 - The Ritz - Dave Smith & The Pilots.

November 6th 1968 - The Ritz - Chicken Shack.

November 8th 1968 - The Ritz - Love Affair.

November 10th 1968 - Pavilion Ballroom - Cupid's Inspiration.

November 11th 1968 - The Ritz - John Mayall's Bluesbreakers with Mick Taylor.

November 15th 1968 - The Ritz - The Alan Bown.

November 20th 1968 - The Ritz - Savoy Brown and his Shake Down Blues Band.

November 22nd 1968 - Winter Gardens - John Mayall's Bluesbreakers with Mick Taylor.

November 23rd 1968 - Winter Gardens - Pentangle.

November 25th 1968 - Oakdale Youth Club - Room.

November 29th 1968 - The Ritz - Steve Miller Delivery.

December 5th 1968 - Royal Ballrooms - Bournemouth Technical College Student's Union Xmas Dance - Pink Floyd / Status Quo / Room.

December 6th 1968 - The Ritz - Black Sabbath.

December 7th 1968 - The Ritz - The Sweet.

December 8th 1968 - Moordown Baptist Church - Cliff Richards.

December 13th 1968 - The Ritz - The Village Blues Band.

December 14th 1968 - The Ritz - The Trifle.

December 17th 1968 - Poole Technical College Student's Union Xmas Dance held at The Ritz - The Nice / Savoy Brown / Pete Lain.

January 27th 1969 - The Ritz - John Mayall's Bluesbreakers with Mick Taylor.

January 31st 1969 - The Ritz - Rainbow Ffolly.

February 1st 1969 - The Ritz - Yes.

February 25th 1969 - The Ritz - Peter Green's Fleetwood Mac.

February 28th 1969 - Winter Gardens - Renaissance (Ex-Yardbird's Keith Relf and Jim McCarty's band).

March 21st 1969 - The Ritz - Mick Abrahams Blues Band.

March 28th 1969 - The Ritz - Taste.

March 30th 1969 - Pavilion Ballroom - Shy Limbs / Tony Blackburn & Band.

April 2nd 1969 - The Pavilion Ballroom - The Who / Third Ear Band / The Embers.

April 19th 1969 - The Ritz - Brother's Bung / The Swinging Clink.

April 25th 1969 - The Ritz - Room.

May 2nd 1969 - The Ritz - Room.

May 15th 1969 - Royal Ballrooms - Bournemouth Municipal College 'May Ball' - The Equals / The Alan Bown / Blossom Toes.

May 16th 1969 - The Ritz - Colosseum.

May 30th 1969 - The Ritz - Howlin' Wolf / John Dummer Blues Band / Room.

June 21st 1969 - The Ritz - Audience.

August 30th 1969 - The Pavilion Ballroom - The Who / Bram Stoker.

September 5th 1969 - The Ritz - Liverpool Scene.

September 12th 1969 - The Ritz - Clouds.

September 19th 1969 - The Ritz - Hard Meat.

September 26th 1969 - The Ritz - Village.

October 3rd 1969 - The Ritz - The Third Ear Band.

October 10th 1969 - The Ritz - Pete Brown & Piblokto.

October 14th 1969 - Poole Technical College - The Edgar Broughton Band / Caravan / Prayer of Hades.

October 17th 1969 - The Ritz - Gypsy.

October 18th 1969 - The Ritz - Stone The Crows.

October 24th 1969 - The Ritz - Jody Grind.

October 31st 1969 - The Ritz - Junior's Eyes.

November 2nd 1969 - Pavilion Ballroom - Zoot Money.

November 7th 1969 - The Ritz - The Strawbs.

November 14th 1969 - The Ritz - Julian's Treatment.

November 16th 1969 - Pavilion Ballroom - Slade.

November 21st 1969 - The Ritz - The Edgar Broughton Band.

November 22nd 1969 - Winter Gardens - John Mayall (no longer known as The Bluesbreakers, with Harvey Mandell on guitar).

December 5th 1969 - The Ritz - Van Der Graff Generator.

December 12th 1969 - The Ritz - Colosseum.

December 26th 1969 - The Ritz - Principle Edwards Magic Theatre.

January 24th 1970 - Winter Gardens - Renaissance.

February 6th 1970 - Winter Gardens - The Nice.

April 24th 1970- Boscombe Ballrooms - Collosseum.

May 2nd 1970 - Winter Gardens - Rare Bird.

May 21st 1970 - The Ritz - Black Sabbath.

June 18th 1970 - Pavilion Ballroom - Colosseum.

July 3rd 1970 - Winter Gardens - Marmalade.

August 18th 1970 - Pavilion Ballroom - Derek & The Dominoes.

August 28th 1970 - Pavilion Ballroom - The Kinks.

October 7th 1970 - Winter Gardens - Derek & The Dominoes / Brett Marvin & The Thunderbolts.

October 20th 1970 - Winter Gardens - Emerson Lake & Palmer.

November 1st 1970 - Winter Gardens - Ten Years After.

November 4th 1970 - Winter Gardens - Ginger Baker's Air Force.

November 6th 1970 - Winter Gardens - Deep Purple.

November 20th 1970 - Chelsea Village - Marmalade.

November 21st 1970 - Winter Gardens - Family.

November 27th 1970 - Winter Gardens - T Rex.

December 6th 1970 - Pavilion Ballroom - Keef Hartley.

December 14th 1970 - Chelsea Village - The Tremeloes.

January 31st 1971 - Winter Gardens - The Faces.

February 1st 1971 - The George Hotel, Poole - Team Dokus.

February 4th 1971 - The Anchor at Shapwick pub, Shapwick - Team Dokus.

February 13th 1971 - Winter Gardens - Van Der Graff Generator.

March 5th 1971 - Winter Gardens - Jethro Tull.

March 10th 1971 - Winter Gardens - Yes.

April 6th 1971 - Winter Gardens - Emerson Lake & Palmer.

April 16th 1971 - Winter Gardens - Mott The Hoople.

April 16th 1971 - Chelsea Village - Marmalade.

April 20th 1971 - Winter Gardens - Electric Light Orchestra.

April 21st 1971 - Winter Gardens - Caravan / Barclay James Harvest / Gringo.

April 24th 1971 - The Ritz - Groundhogs.

June 5th 1971 - The Hive Disco - (Previously The Ritz) - Thin Lizzy.

August 14th 1971 - Starkers Boscombe - Canned Heat / Thin Lizzy.

August 19th 1971 - Starkers Boscombe - Status Quo.

October 8th 1971 - Royal Ballrooms, Boscombe - The Faces / Thin Lizzy.

October 16th 1971 - Winter Gardens - King Crimson.

November 26th 1971 - Winter Gardens - Elton John.

November 27th 1971 - Poole College - Uriah Heep.

December 2nd 1971 - Starkers Ballroom, Boscombe - Led Zeppelin.

January 22nd 1972 - Winter Gardens - Pink Floyd.

February 8th 1972 - Chelsea Village - Thin Lizzy / Arrival.

February 11th 1972 - Royal Ballrooms - Status Quo.

February 11th 1972 - Winter Gardens - Black Sabbath.

April 5th 1972 - Winter Gardens - John Mayall / Matching Mole.

May 26th 1972 - Winter Gardens - Uriah Heep.

June 2nd 1972 - The Old Harry, Poole - Team Dokus.

July 20th 1972 - Boscombe Free Festival - Hawkwind.

August 10th 1972 - Boscombe Royal Ballrooms - Hawkwind.

August 13th 1972 - Winter Gardens - Genesis.

August 17th 1972 - Starkers Boscombe - Status Quo.

August 20th 1972 - Chelsea Village - The Strawbs / Thin Lizzy.

August 24th 1972 - Starkers Boscombe - Uriah Heep.

October 10th 1972 - The Hive Disco - Thin Lizzy.

October 22nd 1972 - Chelsea Village - Status Quo / Byzantium.

November 8th 1972 - Winter Gardens - Slade / Thin Lizzy.

November 10th 1972 - Winter Gardens - Emerson Lake & Palmer.

November 26th 1972 - Winter Gardens - King Crimson.

December 3rd 1972 - Bournemouth Hard Rock - Hawkwind.

January 16th 1973 - Bournemouth Hard Rock - Chuck Berry.

March 17th 1973 - Winter Gardens - Elton John.

April 13th 1973 - Winter Gardens - Roxy Music.

May 11th 1973 - Winter Gardens - Barclay James Harvest.

May 15th 1973 - Winter Gardens - Paul McCartney & Wings.

May 25th 1973 - Winter Gardens - Ziggy Stardust & The Spider's From Mars.

June 12th 1973 - Winter Gardens - Uriah Heep.

September 29th 1973 - Chequers, Lytchett Matravers - Beachcombers.

September 30th 1973 - Bournemouth Hardrock - Family.

October 12th 1973 - Winter Gardens - Genesis.

October 19th 1973 - Winter Gardens - Lindisfarne.

November 6th 1973 - Winter Gardens - Roxy Music.

November 7th 1973 - Winter Gardens - Groundhogs.

November 10th 1973 - Winter Gardens - Uriah Heep / The Heavy Metal Kids.

November 16th and 17th 1973 - Winter Gardens - Yes.

November 19th 1973 - Winter Gardens - The Faces / Long John Baldry.

November 21st 1973 - Winter Gardens - Rory Gallagher / Strider.

November 30th 1973 - Winter Gardens - Mott the Hoople / Queen.

January 19th 1974 - Winter Gardens - Hawkwind.

March 27th 1974 - Winter Gardens - Mott The Hoople.

April 24th 1974 - Winter Gardens - Mick Ronson Band.

May 10th 1974 - Winter Gardens - Status Quo / Montrose.

May 19th 1974 - Winter Gardens - Deep Purple.

May 31st 1974 - Winter Gardens - Black Sabbath.

October 10th 1974 - Winter Gardens - Status Quo.

November 26th 1974 - Winter Gardens - Mott The Hoople / Sparks.

December 1st 1974 - Winter Gardens - Golden Earring / Lynyrd Skynyrd.

December 13th 1974 - Winter Gardens - Uriah Heep.

March 22nd 1975 - Winter Gardens - 10cc.

May 2nd 1975 - Winter Gardens - Planet Gong / Global Village Trucking Company.

June 11th 1975 - Winter Gardens - Hawkwind.

August 26th 1975 - Bournemouth Hard Rock - Motorhead.

September 2nd 1975 - Village Bowl - Thin Lizzy.

October 7th 1975 - Winter Gardens - Leo Sayer.

November 26th 1975 - Winter Gardens - The Moody Blues.

March 8th 1976 - Winter Gardens - Thin Lizzy.

March 12th 1976 - Winter Gardens - Hawkwind.

March 17th 1976 - Winter Gardens - Procol Harum.

May 21st 1976 - Winter Gardens - Sensational Alex Harvey Band.

October 27th 1976 - Winter Gardens - Barclay James Harvest.

December 7th 1976 - Village Bowl - The Sex Pistols, The Damned and The Clash. (The proposed Bournemouth date of The Sex Pistol's 'Anarchy In The UK' tour, but after the Bill Grundy TV appearance and the resulting publicity, The Sex Pistol's pulled out of the tour and soon after The Clash did likewise. So The Damned took on all of the tour dates as headliners.)

December 12th 1976 - Winter Gardens - Hawkwind.

February 28th 1977 - Village Bowl - AC/DC.

October 14th 1977 - Winter Gardens - Dr. Feelgood.

November 9th 1977 - Winter Gardens - The Clash.

November 30th 1977 - Winter Gardens - Thin Lizzy.

December 13th 1977 - Village Bowl - The Damned.

February 2nd 1978 - Tiffany's - Radio Stars.

February 3rd 1978 - Village Bowl - Squeeze.

February16th 1978 - Village Bowl - Eddie & The Hot Rods / Radio Stars.

April 10th 1978 - Poole Arts Centre - Climax Blues Band / Dire Straits.

May 23rd 1978 - Village Bowl - AC/DC.

June 3rd 1978 - Winter Gardens - Blue Oyster Cult.

June 6th 1978 - Winter Gardens - Japan.

September 21st 1978 - Village Bowl - Tom Robinson Band.

October 1st 1978 - Winter Gardens - The Shadows.

October 5th 1978 - Village Bowl - Paul Kossoff's Crawler.

October 17th 1978 - Winter Gardens - Squeeze.

October 18th 1978 - Winter Gardens - Dr Feelgood.

October 19th 1978 - Village bowl - Siouxsie & The Banshees.

October 22nd 1978 - Poole Arts Centre - Motorhead.

October 27th 1978 - Poole Arts Centre - Hawklords

October 30th 1978 - Winter Gardens - Wishbone Ash.

November 7th 1978 - Winter Gardens - Buzzcocks / Subway Sect.

November 9th 1978 - Village Bowl - The Clash / The Slits.

November 15th 1978 - Winter Gardens - 'The Be Stiff Tour' with Wreckless Eric / Rachel Sweet / Lene Lovich / Jonah Lewie.

November 15th 1978 - Poole Arts Centre - Judas Priest.

November 22nd 1978 - Village Bowl - The Clash / The Slits / The Innocents.

November 23rd 1978 - Village Bowl - Squeeze.

December 11th 1978 - Poole Arts Centre - Frankie Miller's Full House.

December 12th 1978 - Poole Arts Centre - Lindisfarne / Chris Rea.

January 28th 1979 - Poole Arts Centre - The Sensational Alex Harvey Band.

March 9th 1979 - Winter Gardens - Uriah Heep.

March 11th 1979 - Poole Arts Centre - The Tina Turner Review.

April 2nd 1979 - Poole Arts Centre - Kate Bush.

April 7th 1979 - Winter Gardens - Thin Lizzy / The Vipers.

October 24th 1979 - Winter Gardens - The Undertones / Ten Pole

Tudor.

November 2nd 1979 - Winter Gardens - The Buzzcocks / Joy Division.

December 8th 1979 - Winter Gardens - Motorhead.

February 24th 1980 - Poole Arts Centre - Uriah Heep.

March 24th 1980 - Winter Gardens - The Undertones / Moondog.

March 26th 1980 - Winter Gardens - Genesis.

May 6th 1980 - Winter Gardens - Mike Oldfield.

October 26th 1980 - Poole Arts Centre - Hawkwind.

November 22nd 1980 - Poole Arts Centre - Uriah Heep.

Terms of Reference:-

Books:
The Eric Clapton Scrapbook by Mark Roberty - Citadel Press.
The Tapestry Of Delights - The Comprehensive Guide to British Music of the Beat, R&B, Psychedelic and Progressive Eras 1963-1976 by Vernon Joynson - Borderline Productions.
Pictures Of An Exhibitionist by Keith Emerson - John Blake Publishing.
The Illustrated Collector's Guide To Motorhead by Alan Burridge - Collector's Guide Publishing.
Cream by Chris Welch - Balafon Books.
Al Stewart - The True Life Adventures of a Folk Rock Troubadour by Neville Judd - Helter Skelter Publishing.
The Alan Bown Set - Before And Beyond by Jeff Bannister - Banland Publishing Ltd.
Keep It Together! - Cosmic Boogie with The Deviants and The Pink Fairies by Rich Deakin - Headpress.
Strange Brew: Eric Clapton and the British Blues Boom 1965-1970 by Christopher Hjort - Jaw Bone Books.
Cream - How Eric Clapton Took The World By Storm by Dave Thompson - Virgin Books.

Newspapers, Magazines, Memorabilia and Microfilm:
Bournemouth Library (Heritage Zone).
Bournemouth Daily Echo.
Borough of Poole Waterfront Museum.
Classic Rock magazine Issue 114 December 2007.
The BourneBeat Hotel & Bar, Priory Road, Bournemouth.

Photos and Memorabilia (used by permission of):
*Jacqueline Ryan at The Troggs Fan Club for copies of my original Cheddar Caves (22th May1966) and Bournemouth Winter Gardens (17th March 1967) photos, entrusted to her Troggs Archives.
*Roy Stockley for the archive photo of Team Dokus.

*Keith Pearce for The Dictator's and Infantes Jubilate photos and memorabilia.

*Bernie James & Gren Fraser for the Elias Hulk material.

*Roy Putt for the Room 'Pre-Flight' album sleeve artwork.

*Steve Edge for the Room Press Photo.

*Roderick Jones at Panama Music Ltd and Tony Bronsdon for the Bram Stoker images.

*Dave Robinson at the Bourne Beat Bar for the posters, The Ritz photo and other memorabilia.

Internet Sources:

www.answers.com

www.iris.dti.ne.jp

www.greglake.com

www.heritage.co.uk

www.marmalade-skies.co.uk

www.thin-lizzy.net/

www.ledzeppelin.com

www.ac-dc.net

www.fmlegacy.com

www.thewholive.de

http://myweb.tiscali.co.uk/hawkwind

http://en.wikipedia.org

www.my-generation.org.uk/Troggs/

http://roomprogressive.blogspot.com

www.bramstoker.uk.com and www.digimixrecords.com

Personal thanks:

Eric Billett, Eddie Evans, Keith Pearce, Dave Robinson, Roy Stockley, Bernie James, Roy Putt, Steve Edge, Roderick Jones, Tony Bronsden, Richard Burridge, Kevin Hannam, Peter Stickland, Alan Plummer, Terry Best, Jon Kremer, Mick Tarrant, John Bongard, Terry Meads, Nick Churchill, Jane & Richard Martin at Natula, Jacqueline Ryan, Jane Burridge, Rob Richardson, Brian Tawn, Richard Tong, Jill Maidment.

Many local bands may feel they were 'missed out' of this publication. If there is enough response, there may be a follow-up book 'A to Z of Bournemouth Area Bands'.

Email the band photo and details to alan.burridge1@ntlworld.com. You can have gigged in the area in the past or the present, this is where your band can be included in a book rather than be forgotten!